Lecture Notes in Computer Science 7228

Commenced Publication in 1973
Founding and Former Series Editors:
Gerhard Goos, Juris Hartmanis, and Jan van Leeuwen

T0242217

Yun Q. Shi (Editor-in-Chief)
Stefan Katzenbeisser (Guest Editor)

Transactions on Data Hiding and Multimedia Security VIII

Special Issue on Pattern Recognition for IT Security

Springer

Editor-in-Chief

Yun Q. Shi
New Jersey Institute of Technology
University Heights, Newark, NJ 07102-1982, USA
E-mail: shi@njit.edu

Guest Editor

Stefan Katzenbeisser
Technical University Darmstadt
Hochschulstrasse 10, 64289 Darmstadt, Germany
E-mail: katzenbeisser@seceng.informatik.tu-darmstadt.de

ISSN 0302-9743 (LNCS)   e-ISSN 1611-3349 (LNCS)
ISSN 1864-3043 (TDHMS)   e-ISSN 1864-3051 (TDHMS)
ISBN 978-3-642-31970-9   e-ISBN 978-3-642-31971-6
DOI 10.1007/978-3-642-31971-6

Springer Heidelberg Dordrecht London New York

CR Subject Classification (1998): K.6.5, E.3, E.4, D.4.6, I.5, I.4

Typesetting: Camera-ready by author, data conversion by Scientific Publishing Services, Chennai, India

Printed on acid-free paper

Springer is part of Springer Science+Business Media (www.springer.com)

Guest Editorial Preface

Special Issue on Pattern Recognition for IT Security

Graphical data, such as images or video streams, are of growing importance in several disciplines of IT security. Examples range from biometric authentication over digital image forensics to visual passwords and CAPTCHAs. Consequently, methods of image analysis and pattern recognition are increasingly used in security-critical applications. Still, there is a significant gap between the methods developed by the pattern recognition community and their uptake by security researchers.

In an attempt to close this gap, a workshop on Pattern Recognition for IT Security was held on September 21, 2010, in Darmstadt, Germany, in conjunction with the 32nd Annual Symposium of the German Association for Pattern Recognition (DAGM 2010). The session was chaired by Jana Dittmann (Otto-von-Guericke Universität Magdeburg), Claus Vielhauer (Fachhochschule Brandenburg) and Stefan Katzenbeisser (Technische Universität Darmstadt).

This special issue contains five selected papers that were presented at the workshop and that demonstrate the broad range of security-related topics that utilize graphical data. Contributions explore the security and reliability of biometric data, the power of machine learning methods to differentiate forged images from originals, the effectiveness of modern watermark embedding schemes and the use of information fusion in steganalysis.

We hope that the papers in this special issue are of interest and inspire future interdisciplinary research between the security and graphics communities.

March 2012   Stefan Katzenbeisser

Table of Contents

Exploiting Relative Entropy and Quality Analysis in Cumulative Partial Biometric Fusion

Hisham Al-Assam, Ali Abboud, Harin Sellahewa, and Sabah Jassim

Department of Applied Computing, University of Buckingham, United Kingdom
{hisham.al-assam,ali.abboud,harin.sellahewa,
sabah.jassim}@buckingham.ac.uk

Abstract. Relative Entropy (RE) of individual's biometric features is the amount of information that distinguishes the individual from a given population. This paper presents an analysis of RE measures for face biometric in relation to accuracy of face-based authentication, and proposes a RE-based partial face recognition scheme that fuses face regions according to their RE-ranks. We establish that different facial feature extraction techniques (FET) result in different RE values, and compare RE values in PCA features with those for a number of wavelet subband features at different levels of decomposition. We demonstrate that for each of the FETs there is a strong positive correlation between RE and authentication accuracy, and that increased image quality results in increased RE and increased authentication accuracy for all FETs. In fact, severe image quality degradation may result in more than 75% drop in RE values. We also present a regional version of these investigations in order to determine the facial regions that have more influence on accuracy and RE values, and propose a partial face recognition that fuses in a cumulative manner horizontal face regions according to their RE-ranks. We argue that the proposed approach is not only useful when parts of facial images are unavailable but also it outperforms the use of the full face images. Our experiments show that the required percentage of facial images for achieving the optimal performance of face recognition varies from just over 1% to 45% of the face image depending on image quality whereas authentication accuracy improves significantly especially for low quality face images.

1 Introduction

Biometrics are physiological and behavioural characteristics that can be used to automatically identify a person. Face is one of the most desired biometrics for unconstrained and unsupervised person identification. A vital process of a face biometric system is the extraction of discriminatory features from a given face image that can be used to identify the person in the given face image or verify a claimed identity. The most common approaches to face recognition consider the entire face image for feature extraction. Typical methods include Eigenfaces [1] and Fisherfaces [2] which use statistical techniques to find an optimal representation in a lower-dimensional face space for a given set of face images. However, the accuracy of these approaches is

Y.Q. Shi (Ed.): Transactions on DHMS VIII, LNCS 7228, pp. 1–18, 2012.

affected by global phenomena such as varying lighting conditions in unconstrained environments. Local feature based approaches [3] aim to extract discriminating features from regions/patches surrounding facial features such as eyes, nose and mouth. Local feature based approaches are invariant to global changes and leads to better recognition accuracy under varying conditions compared to global approaches, but they rely on the accurate location of the specified facial feature. For a variety of applications, interest is growing in expanding these local-feature based face recognition into cases where parts of the face could be occluded or of severely degraded quality. The term partial face recognition refers to such cases, and it is of great interest to forensics, when only parts of the face are available after some accidents such as fire or explosion, and in surveillance applications where only partial faces are recorded. Recently few approaches have been proposed for recognizing faces from partial face images. In [4], radial basis function networks were used to extract and recognize partial face images while the authors in [5] proposed the use of heterogeneous face recognition in which near infrared face videos containing partial faces (probe images) are matched against the visual images of full faces (target images).

Moreover, attention has been given recently to local window based approaches where the entire face image is first partitioned into a set of overlapping/non-overlapping regions and features are extracted from each local region, which are then combined into a single feature representation. Local Binary Patterns [6] and Local Ternary Patterns [7] are two such examples. However, these techniques give equal consideration for each local region in terms of their contribution to the overall recognition, irrespective of the amount of discriminative information in each region.

In information theory, Shannon entropy measures the uncertainty of a random variable. Biometric Entropy, as a special case, describes the inherent differences of population biometric samples, and quantifies their information content [8]. Biometric data is typically represented by a feature vector extracted by one or more Feature Extraction Techniques (FETs). Two factors that should be taken into consideration when measuring biometric entropy are: 1) similarity of samples across different individuals e.g. all human faces have two eyes, a nose and a mouth and 2) the correlation among the biometric features of the same individual. Relative Entropy (RE) of a user's biometric features [9] quantifies the amount of information that distinguishes the user from a given population (discussed further in section 2.1). Quantifying biometric feature's information content (randomness or uncertainty) can address several questions. For example, are fingerprints, faces, or irises really unique? What are the inherent limits of biometric template size requirements and biometric matcher's performance? In terms of biometric system security and cryptosystem evaluations, how much information does an imposter need to guess to fool the system?

There are several factors that influence the performance of biometric systems, such as face sample's image quality, FETs, pre-processing, and the underlying template protection schemes if used [10], [11]. In this paper, we shall confine our attention to the first two factors: biometric image quality and the underlying FET to investigate their influence on the relationship between face feature vector relative entropy and the authentication accuracy.

Factors affecting biometric sample quality can be classified into four groups [12] [13]: (1) user-related factors: these include physiological (e.g. age) and behavioural factors (e.g. pose) which are difficult to control, (2) user-sensor interaction factors: these include the environmental (e.g. lighting) and operational factors (e.g. user familiarity) which are easier to control than user related factors, (3) acquisition sensor factors: these include the sensor characteristics that affect the biometric sample quality (e.g. resolution), and (4) processing system factors: these include factors related to the biometric processing system after the biometric sample is acquired by a sensor such as (e.g. processing algorithms, data format) and these are the easiest to control. The quality of biometric sample can be considered from three points of view: (1) character: an indicator of inherent physical features, (2) fidelity: a measure of the degree of similarity to reference biometric sample, (3) utility: a reference to the impact on the biometric system performance [12].

Little or no work is reported in the literature on the relation between biometric sample quality and biometric entropy. Youmaran and Adler, [14], introduced a theoretical framework which is somewhat restricted to measure the loss of information due to sample quality degradation. It would be essential to extend such a framework to investigate the relationship between information content extracted by different FETs, accuracy rates, and biometric sample's quality. Moreover, different regions of face images are of different structures but have great deal of similarities across individuals. Hence extending these investigations to include regional structures and different entropy concepts would be beneficial.

In this paper, we investigate the use of relative entropy as a measure to rank blocks or patches of face images in terms of their relevance to authentication accuracy. We shall use different FETs and facial images of different qualities in our evaluation. We shall present a comparative analysis of Relative Entropy, illumination-based image quality and authentication accuracy. Existing partial face recognition schemes use the whole (available) part(s) of the images for recognition while our approach just uses the most discriminative blocks (or features) within each part of face images. Finally, we propose a partial face recognition scheme that fuses in a cumulative manner horizontal face regions according to their RE-ranks. This paper is an extension of the work presented at the Pattern Recognition for IT Security workshop, Darmstadt, Germany. A detail analysis of RE, authentication accuracy and image quality and the RE-based partial face recognition scheme form the main extension of this paper.

The rest of this paper is organized as follows: Section 2 provides is a brief review of background material. In Section 3, we analyse the relationships between REs, sample quality, and biometric authentication accuracy. Section 4 investigates the effect of regional variation of features on relative entropy. Section 5 proposes a new RE-based partial face recognition scheme that fuses face regions according to their RE-ranks and Section 6 is devoted for conclusions and future work.

2   Background

In this section, we briefly describe the three main concepts investigated in this paper (i.e. Relative Entropy, Face Recognition, and Image Quality measures), and review related work and techniques in each case.

2.1   Biometric Entropy Measures

The level of randomness of biometric features is an important factor in determining the uniqueness of one's biometric identity. Therefore, measuring information content of biometric systems has a significant impact on accuracy and security. Daugman in [15] proposed the concept of Discrimination entropy to quantify the correlation among the bits of iris templates (degrees of freedom). Given a specific setting, Daugman found that the randomness/uncertainty in the 2048-bit iris template is 249 uncorrelated bits. Matching the bits of two iris codes of length m is equivalent to running m Bernoulli trials whose probability of success (two aligned bits being the same) is 0.5. Hence the Hamming distance between iris codes is a random variable whose probability density function (PDF) has a binomial distribution. If the m Bernoulli trials are independent, then the PDF would be much sharper and the standard deviation will be small. This is due to the correlation among iris's bits [15]. Discrimination entropy of iris codes can be modeled in terms of the degrees of freedom calculated by the following formula:

$$N = \frac{\rho(1-\rho)}{\sigma^2} \tag{1}$$

where ρ and σ are the mean and standard deviation of Binomial Distribution of IrisCode Hamming distances.

Unfortunately, Discriminative Entropy does not account for the amount of information needed to distinguish a user from a population, i.e. it gives no consideration for inter-class variations. To address this problem, a measure between the two distributions i.e. the inter-class and intra-class variation is needed. In statistics, the distance between two distributions can be quantified using a number of different approaches. One interesting measure is the f-divergence, more specifically the Kullback–Leibler (KL) divergence [16] which is also known as relative entropy, or information for discrimination. KL divergence, D(U‖P), is the distance between two distributions P and U which measures the inefficiency of assuming that the distribution is P when it should be U, [17], and is defined as follows:

$$D(U \parallel P) = \int_x U(x) \log_2 \frac{U(x)}{P(x)} dx \tag{2}$$

Alder [9] has extended this definition to be applied to measure entropy of Biometric data. If the population distribution of a certain biometric trait is assumed to be P and a user distribution is U then D(U ‖ P) is the amount of information that distinguishes the user U from the population. Unlike discriminative entropy, relative entropy can be calculated for each individual user.

To estimate the relative entropy D(U‖P), there is a need to estimate the two distributions p(U) and p(P). In our experiments, we need to estimate the distribution of biometrics features across different samples of a user p(U) and across samples of the population p(P). By approximating the two distributions by two Gaussian distributions, the relative entropy is given by [9]:

$$D(U \parallel P) = k\left(\ln\frac{|2\pi\Sigma_P|}{|2\pi\Sigma_U|} + trace\left((\Sigma_P + T)\Sigma_U^{-1} - I\right) \right) \tag{3}$$

where, $(\mu_U, \Sigma_U), (\mu_P, \Sigma_P)$: The mean and the covariance matrix of p(U) and p(P) respectively, and

$$T = (\mu_U - \mu_P)^t(\Sigma_U - \Sigma_P) \text{ and } k = \log_2\sqrt{e}$$

2.2 Face Recognition

Face recognition remains one of the most challenging tasks in comparison to other biometric-based recognition, and several face recognition schemes have been developed and their performances have been tested. An important part of face recognition is the feature extraction procedure. Here we briefly describe two commonly used feature extraction schemes: PCA and wavelet-based schemes.

Typically, feature extraction schemes transform the face image into a "significantly" lower dimensional subspace from which a feature vector is extracted. The most commonly used dimension reduction method is the Principal Component Analysis (PCA), In [1], Turk and Pentland used the PCA technique to develop the Eigenface recognition scheme, simply by using the "most significant" eigenvalues (i.e. of largest absolute values) of the covariance matrix corresponding to a training set of face images.

Frequency transforms provide valuable tools for signal processing and analysis. Frequency information content conveys richer knowledge about features in signals/images that should be exploited to complement the spatial information. Fourier and wavelet transforms are two examples that have been used with significant success in image processing and analysis tasks including face recognition [18], [19], [20]. The discrete wavelet transform (DWT) is a multi-resolution signal analysis tool that hierarchically decomposes a signal into its low- and high-frequency components allowing one to view the signal's regular patterns as well as its anomalies, [18]. At a resolution level of k, the pyramid scheme decomposes an image I into 3k + 1 subbands (LL$_k$;HL$_k$;LH$_k$;HH$_k$; : : : ;HL$_1$;LH$_1$;HH$_1$), with LL$_k$, being the lowest-pass subband. The subbands LH$_1$ and HL$_1$ contain finest scale wavelet coefficients that get coarser with LL$_k$ being the coarsest. The LL$_k$ subband is considered as the k-level approximation of I, while HL$_k$, LH$_k$, and HH$_k$ captures vertical, horizontal and diagonal features of the image.

Different wavelet decomposition levels and/or wavelet filters yield different face feature vectors and FETs. Each subband of a wavelet transformed face image can be used individually as face feature descriptor. Throughout this paper, the Euclidean distance is used for matching, and the Haar wavelet filter is used for the DWT.

2.3   Universal Image Quality Index (UIQI)

It is a well-known fact that face-biometric verification suffers from significant intra-class variation as a result of variation in recording environment, pose, aging … etc. To understand the relationship between accuracy rates and relative entropy contents of face feature vectors, we need to evaluate accuracy and relative entropy in face biometric authentication under varying recording conditions. The extended Yale-B database provides an excellent testing platform for extreme variation in illumination.

The universal image quality index (UIQI) proposed by Wang and Bovik [21] measures the distortion between original signal and reference image by modelling distortion as combination of three main components: correlation distortion, illumination distortion and contrast distortion. Let

$$X = \{x_i \mid i = 1, 2, \ldots \ldots N\} \ and \ Y = \{y_i \mid i = 1, 2, \ldots N\}$$

be the original and the test images respectively. UIQI is defined as:

$$UIQI = \frac{4 \, \sigma_{xy} \, \bar{X} \, \bar{Y}}{(\sigma^2{}_x + \sigma^2{}_y)[(\bar{x})^2 + (\bar{y})^2]} \tag{4}$$

Where, $\bar{x} = \frac{1}{N} \sum_{i=1}^{N} x_i$, $\bar{y} = \frac{1}{N} \sum_{i=1}^{N} y_i$, $\sigma_x^2 = \frac{1}{N-1} \sum_{i=1}^{N} (x_i - \bar{x})^2$,   and

$\sigma_{xy} = \frac{1}{N-1} \sum_{i=1}^{N} (x_i - \bar{x})(y_i - \bar{y})$

In fact, UIQI is the product of three quality measures reflecting these components, respectively as given in equation (5).

$$Q = \frac{\sigma_{xy}}{\sigma_x \sigma_y} \bullet \frac{2 \, \overline{xy}}{(\bar{x})^2 + (\bar{y})^2} \bullet \frac{2 \sigma_x \sigma_y}{\sigma^2{}_x + \sigma^2{}_y} \tag{5}$$

Here, we only consider the luminance distortion component as given in equation (6).

$$LQI = \frac{2 \, \bar{x} \, \bar{y}}{(\bar{x})^2 + (\bar{y})^2} \tag{6}$$

In practice, the LQI of an image with respect to another reference image is calculated for each window of size 8x8 pixels in the two images, and the average of these entire blocks defines the LQI of the entire image. Based on Extended Yale B face database [22] described below, the reference image used to calculate LQI index is the average face image of all 38 individuals (i.e. the average of the frontal pose and in direct illumination image (P00A+000E+00) of each subject) [23].

2.4 Experimental Dataset and Testing Protocol

The Extended Yale B database, [22], has 38 subjects and each one, in frontal pose, has 64 images captured under different illumination conditions. The total number of images in the database is 2414 images. The images in the database are divided into five subsets according to the direction of the light-source from the camera axis. Samples of images taken from the database are shown in Figure 1.

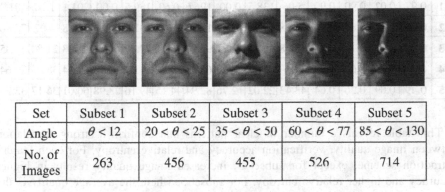

Set	Subset 1	Subset 2	Subset 3	Subset 4	Subset 5
Angle	$\theta < 12$	$20 < \theta < 25$	$35 < \theta < 50$	$60 < \theta < 77$	$85 < \theta < 130$
No. of Images	263	456	455	526	714

Fig. 1. Sample of images for the same person in different illumination subset

To test the proposed RE-based cumulative partial face recognition scheme, the 38 users are divided into two separate portions (18 users each): one is used for development (i.e. creating RE-based ranks), and the other is used for testing (i.e. authentication accuracy evaluation using the RE-based ranks from the development stage). In all experiments, the first three images per user from subset 1 (the extended Yale-B database) were selected as reference images to form the gallery set and all the remaining images were used for matching which is based on the Euclidean distances. For a subset i, if Ni is the number of testing images, then the number of client tests= Ni × 38, and the number of imposter tests= (Ni × 37 × 38) /2. All face images were used without pre-processing.

3 Entropy, Accuracy, and Quality of Whole Face Samples

In this section, facial feature vectors are extracted from the whole face image using five FETs: 4 wavelets subbands (LL4, LH4, HL4, and HH4) and PCA in the spatial domain. The output of applying each of the FETs is a feature vector of size (132), which makes the results of the five FETs comparable.

Table 1 shows the relationship between the biometric Relative Entropies (REs), authentication accuracy represented by the Equal Error Rates (EERs), and biometric sample quality (in terms of LQI). It provides a comparison of the performance of the five FETs for the different subsets of the database.

Table 1. Comparison of authentication accuracy vs. relative entropy for different illumination quality levels

Subsets	Quality				Entropy & Authentication Accuracy									
					LL4(132)		LH4(132)		HL4(132)		HH4(132)		PCA(132)	
	Avg	Std	Min	Max	EER (%)	RE (bits)	EER (%)	RE (bits)	EER (%)	RE (bits)	EER (%)	RE (bits)	EER (%)	RE (bits)
S1	0.97	0.02	0.90	0.99	5.06	138.5	0.00	196.6	0.69	189.5	0.00	201.1	1.70	101.3
S2	0.96	0.02	0.88	0.99	21.58	79.90	1.42	144.7	3.47	132.0	0.08	150.8	4.07	77.86
S3	0.91	0.04	0.78	0.97	34.08	36.46	5.70	92.87	18.11	77.79	4.40	91.88	21.80	43.85
S4	0.79	0.07	0.60	0.89	44.39	14.98	14.20	68.43	39.70	41.45	19.98	59.24	38.65	24.64
S5	0.49	0.09	0.26	0.64	43.43	22.02	12.76	82.94	44.15	49.16	23.98	66.01	36.17	32.23

This table reveals a number of clear patterns that confirm a strong correlation between image quality, verification accuracy and relative entropy. For each feature extraction scheme, except for subset 5, increased image quality results in higher accuracy and higher relative entropy. For subset 5, where the average quality is the lowest, the pattern is not a clear one. All the wavelet-based schemes significantly outperform the PCA scheme in terms of both accuracy rate and relative entropy. Among the wavelet based schemes the HH4 has the best performance when the image quality average is > 0.6 which excludes most of subsets 4 and 5, otherwise the LH4 has best performance if image quality < 0.6. The latter observation can be attributed to the fact that the most significant facial features (i.e. eyes and mouth) have elliptical shapes but predominantly in the horizontal direction, and worsening illumination indices have less effect on horizontal features. Note that, LH4 does highlight horizontal features.

4   Entropy, Accuracy, and Quality of Regional Face Samples

The fact that different facial features (i.e. eyes, nose, mouth, chin, cheeks, and eyebrows) have different structures and are in relatively known locations within the face image, it is necessary to investigate the regional contribution to authentication accuracy and RE values. Here we analyze the face sample quality and entropy across different regions of facial images, and discuss the relationship with authentication accuracy. Since facial features are mostly horizontal, we confine our investigation to vertical regions. Such analysis addresses the question: Is relative entropy distributed uniformly over all regions of the biometric data or do some face regions have higher

RE compared to others? Understanding the distribution of REs across different face regions might help in a number of applications such as adaptive fusion, biometric key generation, and adaptive quality assessment.

Overlapping horizontal windows of size is 8x168 are used for the regional RE analysis of the 192x168 pixel face images. The use of overlapping widows reduces the chance of cutting discriminating features and facilitates reasonable alignment of facial features for all person images. In order to use wavelet-based feature extraction schemes, individual window height must be at least 2k for k^{th} level decomposition. We observed that most individual facial features are contained within 8 rows in the spatial domain, while windows of height 16 would certainly cover more parts or all of two facial features. Hence, the selected window size is (8x168) pixels and the overlap between two successive windows is (6x168) pixels. Hence, 93 overlapped horizontal windows cover the whole face image. This choice limits the level of wavelet decomposition to 3.

First we used LQI to measure the image quality of each window to get a better understanding of the distribution of quality across different regions of face images (i.e. illumination distribution for this database). Figure 2 shows the regional quality variations for each subset of the extended Yale B database. Remarkably this chart illustrates that the quality of each window is affected in the same way in the 5 different subsets of the database even though in each subset these qualities fluctuate across the regions.

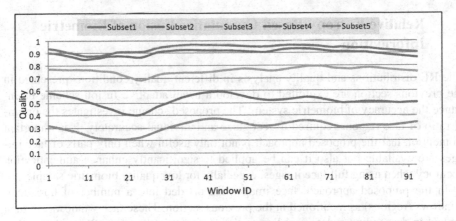

Fig. 2. Quality variations across different overlapped regions in the spatial domain

Figure 3 illustrates the regional relative entropies and authentication accuracy (in terms of EER (%)). Figure 3A and 3B present regional RE and accuracy distributions of LH3 across the different five subsets. The average Equal Error Rates (EER) of all individuals is reported. The regional RE chart of the LH3 shows that the upper part features of the face image has the highest discriminative information (RE), the bottom part face features comes second, and the middle part face features has the lowest information content. This claim is supported by the general trend of authentication accuracy (in terms of EER %) where the upper windows tend to outperform other regions. In other words, the upper part features of the face image contribute more in recognizing different individuals. Moreover, the regional REs decrease sharply as a result to image quality degradations. It can also be seen that detecting the most informative regions is dependent on the underlying FET. For example, (LL3, LH3, and PCA) include more information content in the upper region windows compared to (HL3 and HH4) whereas the latter two include more information content in the bottom region windows as well as in the upper regions. This observation about the RE distribution can be used to improve adaptive fusion of FETs for enhanced accuracy. In adaptive fusion, different weights are given to different components of the fused system and here we should be having a strategy that exploits the regional variations and quality values to dynamically selecting the weights. For brevity of space, we chose to present one detailed regional RE chart of one FET only (i.e. LH3). The other four FETs exhibit a similar pattern.

Figure 3C,3D, and 3E summarise the results by showing EER verses median, maximum, minimum of regional RE respectively of the five FETs (LL3, LH3, HL3, HH3, and PCA), across the five subsets. The median is used instead of the mean for exact mapping to the corresponding EER. The figures show how RE decreases and EER increases when biometric image quality decreases (i.e. moving from subset1 to subset5). The figures also illustrate how different FETs capture different amount of information, and achieve different recognition accuracy at different regions of face biometric.

5   Relative Entropy-Based Cumulative Fusion of Biometric Information

The RE distributions and quality analysis in different quality conditions presented in the previous section are exploited to develop a novel adaptive fusion scheme to enhance the accuracy of biometric system. The proposed scheme investigates the optimal ratio of face regions required to recognize an individual accurately. It is important to mention that the proposed approach is not only useful when only parts of face images are available but also it can be applied to significantly enhance authentication accuracy when using full face images, especially for low quality biometric samples.

In the proposed approach, face images are divided into a number of horizontal windows (regions) as mentioned in the previous section. These face windows are then ranked in descending order according to their information content (RE) to be used in cumulative way at the recognition stage. In other words, our approach first selects the region with the highest RE and then the region with the next highest RE is fused with first one at the feature level, and so on.

Here, we investigate the use of the proposed RE-based fusion on wavelet subbands in two ways: within a subband fusion and among different multi-subbands fusion. The proposed method can be equally applied to facial feature vectors extracted by any other FETs. For simplicity, non-overlapped horizontal windows are used to avoid the possibility of having redundant representation when applying the feature level fusion.

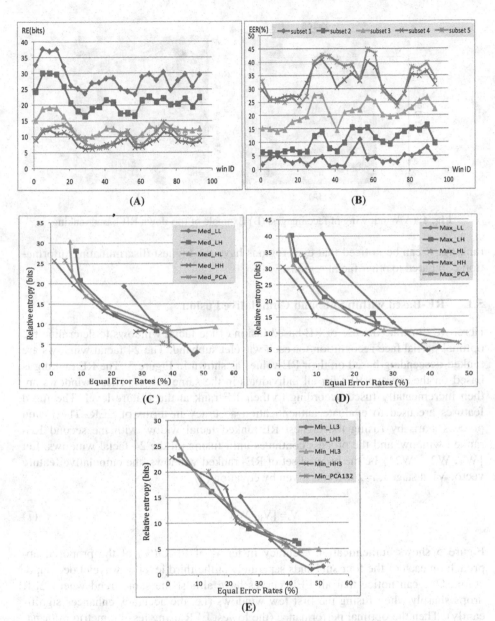

Fig. 3. A and B present Regional RE and accuracy distributions for LH3 across different subsets (win ID axis represents top-down overlapped windows), C, D, and E show EER verses median, maximum, minimum of regional RE respectively for the five FETs across the five subsets

Figure 4(A) shows the horizontal non-overlapped windowing process. The original facial image size is (192x168) pixels and each window is (8x168) pixels which results in a total of 24 windows. Figure 4(B) presents an example of a top-down RE-based

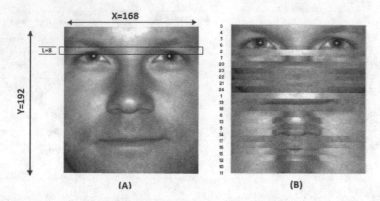

Fig. 4. (A)Windowing of face images, (B) Example of top-down RE-based ranking

ranking. It can be noticed that eyes regions have the highest discriminating information compared to other facial regions.

5.1   RE-Based within Subband Cumulative Fusion

Here, we illustrate the use of RE-based fusion of the facial windows to determine the optimal partial face recognition for each wavelet subband. The 24 facial windows are ranked descending based on their RE values as shown in Figure 5. The RE ranking is based on the average REs for all individuals in the same subset. These windows are then incrementally fused according to their RE rank at the feature level. The fused features are used to evaluate authentication accuracy in terms of EER. The fusion process starts by fusing the highest RE-ranked facial widow with the second RE-ranked window, and the process continues until fusing all the 24 facial windows. Let {W1, W2,.., W24} be the ordered set of RE- ranked windows, the cumulative feature vector Vi at stage i, i=2 to 24, is given by equation (7)

$$V_i = [V_{i-1} \ W_i] \tag{7}$$

Figure 5 shows authentication accuracy in terms of EER (%) of the proposed approach on each of the four subbands separately at the third level of wavelet decomposition. One can notice that all EER curves have almost the same trend where EER drops sharply when fusing the first few windows (i.e. the accuracy enhances significantly). Then the optimal performance (the lowest EER using less biometric information) is achieved somewhere in middle i.e. when using half of the facial windows. It can also be noticed that the optimal performance is different among subbands and subsets. Moreover, once achieving the best performance, EER either stays the same, for example the LH3, HL3, and HH3 subands of first three subsets, or increases monotonically (worse accuracy) in all other cases. In other words, fusing more regions of facial images does not help in improving accuracy, but it might impair recognition accuracy in some cases such as the LL3 subband of all subsets except subset1.

To highlight the benefits of the proposed scheme, the performance of the proposed approach is compared with the performance of the approach that uses whole face images. For brevity of space, Figure 6 only presents the results for LL3 suband across the five subsets. However, the same trend is observed for all other subbands. It can be seen that in all scenarios, using only the most informative regions of face images outperform the use of whole face image in terms of authentication accuracy. Apart from subset1, the optimal performance can be achieved using less than 7 windows out of the 24 (i.e. less than 30% of the whole face image). For subset1, with best image quality, more regions are required to obtain the best performance however RE-based fusion approach still outperforms the whole face image-based scheme.

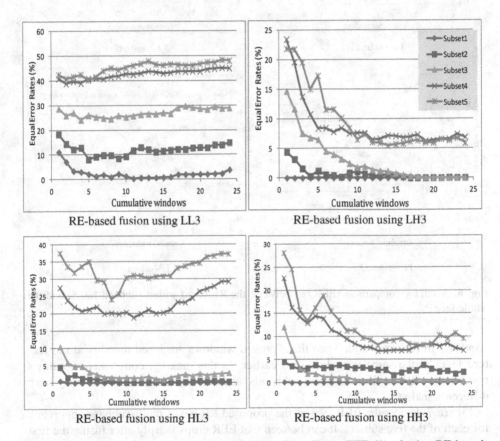

RE-based fusion using LL3   RE-based fusion using LH3

RE-based fusion using HL3   RE-based fusion using HH3

Fig. 5. Face recognition accuracy in terms of Equal Error Rates (EER %) of using RE-based cumulative fusion for the four subbands {LL3, LH3, HL3, and HH3}

5.2   RE-Based Multi-subbands Cumulative Fusion

Here, we propose another scheme for cumulative biometric information fusion which uses all four subbands of a specific wavelet decomposition level (level 3 in this paper). The 96 windows from the four subbands (24x4) are ranked instead of the 24

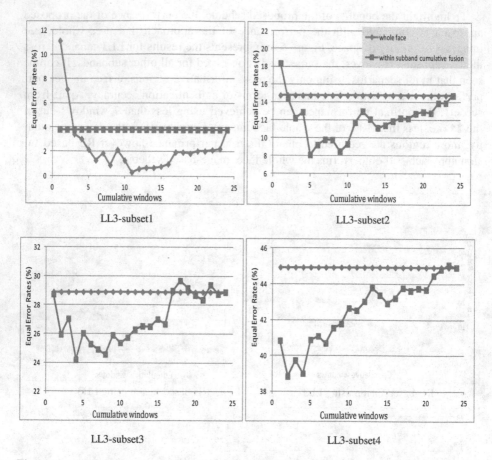

Fig. 6. Accuracy comparison (EER %) between the RE-based within subband fusion and the whole face

windows in each subband. Then these ranked windows are fused together at the feature level in the same way described earlier. In this ranking, consecutive windows may or may not be from different subbands, and also different individuals may have different ranking.

Figure 7 depicts the EER (%) of the proposed RE-based multi-subbands approach for each of the five subsets. It can be seen that EER drops sharply after fusing the first few windows.

To gain a better insight into the effectiveness of the proposed multi-subbands RE-based fusion approach, we compare the authentication accuracy (in terms of EER) of the proposed approach with the authentication accuracy of the whole face images as illustrated in Figure 8. One can observe that in all subsets, using only the most informative regions outperform the use of whole face image in terms of authentication accuracy. In fact, adopting the proposed approach may lead to significant improve-ment in authentication accuracy in subset 3, subset 4, and subset 5 where the image quality is significantly poor. Table 2 summarizes the results of the multi-subbands RE-based fusion and whole face image schemes.

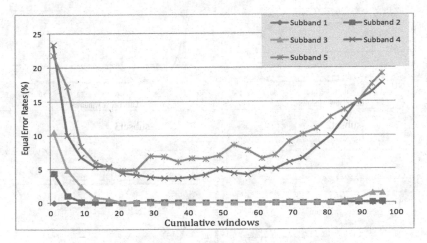

Fig. 7. Multi-subband RE-based fusion

Table 2. Comparing EERs of the proposed RE-based fusion with EERs of the whole face for different subsets of extended Yale-B

	Subset1	Subset2	Subset3	Subset4	Subset5	Average
EER(whole face)	0.00	0.15	1.46	17.79	19.17	7.71
Optimal EER(multi-subbands fusion)	0.00	0.00	0.00	3.43	4.44	1.57
Optimal Percentage of the face needed to recognize individuals	1.04%	10.42%	44.79%	32.29%	20.83%	21.21%

The table shows that the proposed approach significantly enhances the authenti-caion accuracy in terms of EER. In fact, the proposed RE-based fusion scheme out-performs the use of full facial image especiaally for low quality face images.The EER for drops from (1.46%) to (0%), from (17.79%) to (3.43%), and from (19.17%) to (4.44%) for subset 3, subset 4 and subset 5 respectively. The table also shows that the average percentage of the face regions required to recognize each individual is around 21% (ranging from just over 1% to around 45% according to the quality of the under-lying facial images) and the average EER might drop from (7.71%) to (1.57%) when adopting the proposed approach.

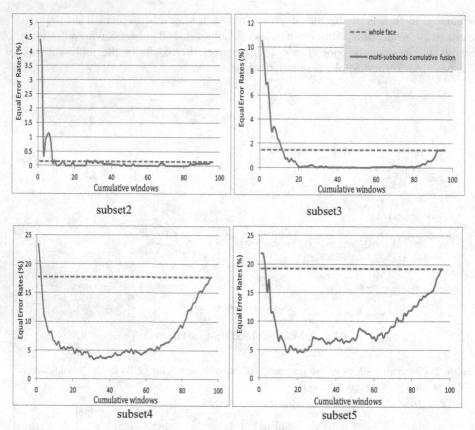

Fig. 8. Accuracy comparison (EER %) between the cumulative multi-subbands RE-based fusion and the whole face

6   Conclusions

We have investigated the relationship between the level of randomness in face biometric as represented by relative entropy (RE), and the accuracy rates for a number of face recognition schemes under variant illumination conditions. We have demonstrated a strong correlation between RE values and accuracy rates that holds for different image quality levels and different recognition schemes. The RE values are dependent on the recognition scheme with wavelet based ones all outperforming the PCA scheme. Except for the lowest quality level, the RE value increases as image quality improves. Similar patterns have been revealed when regional RE's and accuracy rates were investigated, and the results demonstrate that the middle region of the face has less randomness than the upper or the lower part of the face. Furthermore, we proposed a RE-based partial face recognition that fuses, in a cumulative manner, horizontal face regions according to their RE-ranks. We have demonstrated that the proposed approach is not only useful when parts of facial images are available but also it outperforms the use of the full face images. Our experiments show that the percentage of face area needed to achieve the optimal performance varies from just over 1% to 45% of the face image depending on the quality of the underlying facial image. Also, the authentication accuracy significantly improves, especially for low quality images, e.g. EERs drop from 1.46 %, 17.79 %, and 19.17% based on the whole face images to 0.0%, 3.43%, 4.44% for subset 3, subset4 and subset 5 respectively using the proposed partial face recognition scheme when only the highest ranked face areas are used for authentication. This paper has focused on one type of quality factor, the illumination factor. In our future work, we shall consider other biometric quality factors such as pose and resolution to create multiple ranking indices where the ranking index is adaptively selected at the authentication stage by assessing the quality vector of the presented biometric sample.

References

1. Pentland, M., Turk, A.P.: Face Recognition Using Eigenfaces. In: IEEE Conference on Computer Vision and Pattern Recognition (1991)
2. Belhumeur, P.N., Hespanha, J.P., Kriegman, D.J.: Eigenfaces vs. fisherfaces: Recognition using class specific linear projection. IEEE Trans. on Pattern Analysis and Machine Intelligence 19(7), 711–720 (1997)
3. Penev, P.S., Atick, J.J.: Local feature analysis: A general statistical theory for object representation. Network: Computation in Neural Systems 7(3), 477–500 (1996)
4. Gutta, S., Philomin, V., Trajkovic, M.: An investigation into the use of partial-faces for face recognition. In: International Conference on Automatic Face and Gesture Recognition, pp. 33–38 (2002)
5. Yi, D., Liao, S., Lei, Z., Sang, J., Li, S.Z.: Partial Face Matching between Near Infrared and Visual Images in MBGC Portal Challenge. In: Tistarelli, M., Nixon, M.S. (eds.) ICB 2009. LNCS, vol. 5558, pp. 733–742. Springer, Heidelberg (2009)
6. Ahonen, T., Hadid, A., Pietikäinen, M.: Face description with local binary patterns: Application to face recognition. IEEE Trans. on Pattern Analysis and Machine Intelligence, 2037–2041 (2006)
7. Tan, X., Triggs, B.: Enhanced local texture feature sets for face recognition under difficult lighting conditions. In: Proceedings of the 3rd International Conference on Analysis and Modelling of Faces and Gestures, pp. 168–182 (2007)
8. Li, S.Z.: Encyclopaedia of Biometrics. Springer (2009)
9. Adler, A., Youmaran, R., Loyka, S.: Towards a Measure of Biometric Information. In: The Canadian Conference on Electrical and Computer Engineering (CCECE), pp. 210–213 (2006)
10. Al-Assam, H., Sellahewa, H., Jassim, S.A.: Lightweight approach for biometric template protection. In: Proceedings of SPIE (2009)
11. Jassim, S., Al-Assam, H., Sellahewa, H.: Improving performance and security of biometrics using efficient and stable random projection techniques. In: Proc. 6th International Symposium on Image and Signal Processing and Analysis, ISPA (2009)
12. Castillo, O.Y.G.: Survey about Facial Image Quality. Fraunhofer Institute for Computer Graphics Research, 10–15 (2005)
13. Yen, R.: New Approach for Measuring Facial Image Quality. In: Biometric Quality Workshop II in Proc. National Institute of Standards and Technology, pp. 7–8 (2007)

14. Youmaran, R., Adler, A.: Measuring biometric sample quality in terms of biometric infor-
    mation. In: Biometric Consortium Conference, 2006 Biometrics Symposium, pp. 1–6
    (2006)
15. Daugman, J.: The importance of being random: statistical principles of iris recognition.
    Pattern Recognition 36(2), 279–291 (2002)
16. Kullback, S., Leibler, R.A.: On information and sufficiency. The Annals of Mathematical
    Statistics 22(1), 79–86 (1951)
17. Cover, T., Thomas, J.: Elements of information theory, 2nd edn. (2006)
18. Lades, M., Vorbrüggen, J.C., Buhmann, J., Lange, J., von der Malsburg, C., Wurtz, R.P.,
    Konen, W.: Distortion Invariant Object Recognition in the Dynamic Link Architecture.
    IEEE Trans. Computers 42(3), 300–311 (1993)
19. Jassim, S.A., Sellahewa, H.: A wavelet-based approach to face verification/recognition. In:
    Proc. SPIE, vol. 5986, p. 77 (2005)
20. Dai, D.-Q., Yuen, P.C.: Wavelet-Based 2-Parameter Regularized Discriminant Analysis
    for Face Recognition. In: Proc. AVBPA Int'l Conf. Audio and Video-Based Biometric
    Person Authentication, pp. 137–144 (2003)
21. Bovik, A.C., Wang, Z.: A Universal Image Quality Index. IEEE Signal Processing Let-
    ters 9(3), 81–84 (2002)
22. Georghiades, A.S., Belhumeur, P.N., Kriegman, D.J.: From Few to Many: Generative
    Models for Recognition under Variable Pose and Illumination. IEEE Trans. on Pattern
    Analysis and Machine Intelligence 23(6), 643–660 (2001)
23. Sellahewa, H., Jassim, S.: Image-Quality-Based Adaptive Face Recognition. IEEE Trans.
    on Instrumentation and Measurement 59(4), 805–813 (2010)

Improving Reliability of Biometric Hash Generation through the Selection of Dynamic Handwriting Features

Andrey Makrushin[1], Tobias Scheidat[1,2], and Claus Vielhauer[1,2]

[1] Otto-von-Guericke University of Magdeburg, Universitätsplatz 2,
39106 Magdeburg, Germany
[2] University of Applied Sciences Brandenburg, Magdeburger Str. 50,
14770 Brandenburg an der Havel, Germany
makrushin@iti.cs.uni-magdeburg.de,
{scheidat,vielhauer}@fh-brandenburg.de

Abstract. The feature extraction, which is the most critical part of biometric recognition systems, is solely done based on expert knowledge or rather intuitively. Thus, no guaranty could be given that extracted features are suitable for biometric user authentication. Moreover, the expert knowledge could be only applied for a particular quality of raw data or only defined for a particular database. Therefore, the feature analysis is required to estimate the discrimination power of extracted features and automatically eliminate all irrelevant or redundant ones. In order to provide a feature ranking and consequent filtering, authors suggest several heuristics and compare these to each other and to several wrapper approaches. The experiments were done on features extracted from dynamic handwriting data. The comparison of feature subsets is provided based on hash generation performance of quantization based secure sketch algorithm. The experiments show a significant increase of reproduction rates (RR) and decrease of collision rates (CR). After feature selection the CR for the most appropriate written content 'symbol' reduced from 5.04% to 3.44% and the RR grows from 70.57% to 93.59%. Furthermore, the lower number of features ensures the reduction of computational complexity and, thus, classification speed-up.

Keywords: Feature selection, handwriting, biometrics, biometric hashing, fuzzy extractor, secure sketch.

1 Introduction

Apart from the human voice the handwriting is the most commonly used behavioural biometric modality. Handwriting is widely used in forensic science, namely in court cases, to check if an individual is the author of a certain handwritten document. Another well known domain of handwriting-based applications is handwriting recognition, which could be designated as an automatic retrieval of the ground truth of a handwritten document and often associated with optical character recognition (OCR) systems. However, in this work the focus is laid on the third major group of handwriting-based applications – biometric user authentication. The main objective

Y.Q. Shi (Ed.): Transactions on DHMS VIII, LNCS 7228, pp. 19–41, 2012.

here is to identify or to verify a person based on *predefined* handwritten content through comparison of reference and test samples.

In a biometric context, the handwriting is usually associated with the signature recognition. However, the signature as a written content has several disadvantages. The names of the user are usually publicly known, and even an uninformed attacker can guess the signature's shape. Moreover, once the personal signature is compromised, it cannot be changed in an easy way. It will be shown, that other written contents could be more appropriate for user verification.

The most known practical applications, which make use of handwriting-based user verification, are signing of bank documents on digital tablets and signature based login scenarios on tablet PCs or for building entrance.

In contrast to static handwriting data, which is either continuous trajectory of a pen movement on a paper or a digitalized set of points with x/y-coordinates, the dynamic handwriting data contains a time sequence of points. Each point has at least an order, a sampling time and relative x/y-coordinates on the writing surface. Depending on the digital sampling device, characteristics of points can be extended by pressure and pen angles, namely pen azimuth and pen altitude (see figure 1). There are other signals such as height of pen above digitizer, tilt along the x/y-axis, rotation around pen axis, which could be potentially captured, but the appropriate tablets are seldom used in academic research as well as in commercial applications. Practically, x/y-coordinates, pressure, altitude and azimuth are considered as functions of time ($x(t)$, $y(t)$, $p(t)$, $\varphi(t)$, $\theta(t)$) and can be qualified as the basic input data for further processing.

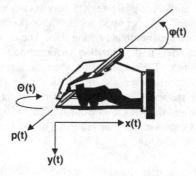

Fig. 1. Basic handwriting signals: $x(t)$ – horizontal pen position, $y(t)$ – vertical pen position, $p(t)$ – pressure, $\varphi(t)$ – altitude, $\theta(t)$ – azimuth (taken from [25])

As well as every other behavioural biometric modality, the handwriting is characterized by very high variations of acquired signals in genuine samples. Pressure, writing angles and shape change under the influence of donor's mood, physical condition and other factors, which are almost unpredictable. This leads to insufficient authentication rates. In order to reduce these variations, stable individual characteristics (further called features) should be derived from acquired signals. Moreover, the features need to be independent from environmental conditions.

Unfortunately, there is no common methodology to define and extract features, which are surely suitable for user authentication. Usually the extraction is done based on formerly collected expert knowledge or rather intuitively. The expert knowledge is usually valid for some domain specific features and could be incomplete or erroneous. In certain cases the resulting features will be completely unsuitable for user authentication. In this sense, the feature extraction could be denoted as a "blind" process and therefore a subsequent feature relevance analysis is essential. There are 131 features considered in this work. The feature extraction is based on empirical research and intuition. Table 1 gives an overview of features and characterizes them depending on signals needed for meaningful extraction.

Table 1. Handwriting features

Feature type	Description	Number
Time-based statistics: t	total time number of (valid) sampling points	1, 2, 30
Static spatial statistics: x, y (time and order independent)	x/y aspect ratios, (normalized) centroid of horizontal/vertical pen position, (normalized) distance between centroid and origin, normalized average velocity in x/y-direction, path length, number of points in special regions (left/right half, top/middle/bottom third etc.), accumulated points' offsets from the left bottom corner in particular time slots, angle between linear regression line and baseline, ratio between area/perimeter of convex hull and area/perimeter of bounding box, number of local x/y-minima/maxima, ratio between the numbers of local x/y-minima and local x/y-maxima, total number of self crossings, and numbers of self crossings sorted by angels, number of intersections with horizontal, vertical and diagonal lines, ratio between the path length and start-end distance/width/height, ratio between the start-centroid distance and centroid-end distance, linearly mapped and accumulated x/y-extremes, average/minimum/maximum number of points within the circle around each sample point, number of the closed areas inside the path, x/y-coordinates of cluster centrionds of signature points	3, 18, 11, 12, 15, 16, 13, 17 26, 27, 31, 32-43, 59-61, 68, 69, 44-55, 58, 62, 65, 70-73, 74, 75, 76, 98-103, 77-85, 86-88, 89, 90-92, 95-97, 107, 108-119
Dynamic spatial statistics: x(t), y(t)	average/minimum/maximum velocity in x/y direction, linearly mapped and accumulated pen acceleration, speed at the inflection points	4, 5, 7-10, 93, 130
Pressure-based statistics: p(t)	number of segments, average/maximum pressure, pen up time, ratio between pen up and pen down time, ratio between accumulated pressure and maximum pressure in pen up/down positions, ratio between area/perimeter of convex hulls around the path segments and area/perimeter of global bounding box, average/minimum/maximum length of contact less movement, average pressure in different pressure clusters, pressure standard deviation	6, 14, 23, 28, 29, 56, 57, 63, 64, 66, 67, 94, 104-106, 120-125, 131
Angles-based statistics: φ(t), θ(t)	average/minimum/maximum altitude/azimuth, average altitude in different pressure clusters	19-22, 24, 25, 126-129

Obviously, not all features are appropriate in each situation. Taking into account digital sampling device and written content, it could be clearly seen that some features do not have any variation through the samples of all users. Therefore, the feature analysis and subsequent selection of the subset of relevant features is a central issue addressed here. It is shown that selection of the features with low intra-class variance and high inter-class variance results in lower user authentication errors.

Another issue considered in this work is the comparison of written contents regarding the user authentication or more precisely hash generation performance. In contrast to physiological biometric traits, the behavioral traits can contain secret knowledge, which means that biometric information is presented in some secret way. Hence, unauthorized verification attempts can be split into random and intentional forgeries, according to the awareness of the attacker about the secret. In order to demonstrate how the secret knowledge and uniqueness of the written content influence verification performance, five different written contents are evaluated in this work. First, the public PIN is proposed. This is a combination of five predefined digits "77993", which are written in a similar manner among people of all nationalities. In this regard, any sample could be considered as an intentional forgery. Next, the secret PIN is proposed. This is a combination of five arbitrary digits from zero to nine. Here, the variability of the written shape between users is evident. Nevertheless, the variance is not high enough, because most donors are used to write digits in a similar way and to provide a short pause and lift the pen after each digit. More variance and uniqueness are contained in the third written content – pseudonym. This one is very similar to the signature. People have been asked to train and to provide a new signature, different to the personal one. This can contain any fictional name. It has been intentionally refrained from capturing personal signatures due to privacy reasons. The amount of uniqueness increases in the fourth written content – symbol. It does not necessarily have to be a text symbol. It could be any kind of drawing. It is very hard for an attacker to reproduce this one correctly, even if the shape of the writing is presented on the tablet. The last written content is an answer to the question "Where are you from?" The text here is usually the name of a city or of a country and can be easily guessed. The variance of the samples is poor, because most donors descent from the same region. Obviously, any other personal question, even with the higher variability of possible answer, can be picked instead of the one mentioned before. Figure 2 shows examples of the considered written contents. Following the [25], the written contents will be referred to as semantics.

(a)   (b)   (c)   (d)   (e)

Fig. 2. Examples of semantics: (a) public PIN, (b) secret PIN, (c) pseudonym, (d) symbol, (e) answer to the question "Where are you from?"

The next important issue discussed in this paper is secure template preservation. A reference database consisting of personal biometric data is of very high interest for criminals. The stolen identity could be used by forgers in a crime scene to cover up the traces or to gain unauthorized access to a secret. From technical point of view, the biometric system designer should guarantee that the templates, stored in the reference database, are irreversible. This means that it is impossible to reconstruct original biometric data from biometric templates.

In order to provide secure template preservation the biometric hashing procedure is proposed. The main idea of biometric hashing is a generation of the individual stable hash value for each user from varying biometric data. Furthermore, the concept of biometric hashing implies a robust hash generation, which means that the same hash should be produced for all biometric samples of a person and clearly dissimilar hashes should be produced for biometric samples of different persons. This fact offers the challenge of combining biometrics and cryptography, because the robust hash can be used as a seed for generation of a personal cryptographic key. As a practical realization of biometric hashing, a secure sketch algorithm for dynamic handwriting proposed in [21] is selected.

To sum up, we would like to emphasize that the focus of this work is laid on improvement of biometric user authentication based on dynamic handwriting, through the selection of relevant handwriting features. The feature selection is examined in conjunction with the specific realization of secure sketch algorithm, proposed in the third section. The authors have investigated the influence of the intelligent feature reduction on the hash generation performance and found out that a reduced feature set leads not only to computational speed-up but also to lower collision and higher reproduction rates.

2   Related Works

The idea of secure preservation of biometric templates and combining of biometrics and cryptography has been one of the topics most discussed in biometric research society during the last years [10]. It is a very attractive perspective for a biometric system to be able to generate cryptographic keys from biometric characteristics. In fact, people do not need to memorize a password phrase or possess a dongle to obtain secured access to a system. However, it is a great challenge to stabilize fuzzy biometric signals providing high reproduction and low collision rates during the biometric hash generation and at the same time to guarantee the perfect secrecy of privacy sensitive data. The theoretical aspects of authentication reliability and secrecy warranty are addressed in [2, 24].

2.1   Biometric Hashing

The general terminology in domain of cryptographic keys generation from noisy data is proposed by Dodis in [4]. The authors introduce the term fuzzy extractor as a primary primitive for the solving of the mentioned problem. The fuzzy extractor comprises two procedures: secure sketch algorithm and strong extractor. Secure sketch algorithm is used for the generation of helper data (sketch) from reference samples in the enrollment stage and for the reconstruction of reference data from a test sample in the authentication stage, making use of helper data. Strong extractor creates the secret key from the original or reproduced reference data. Helper data is considered as public information and can be available for attackers. Strong extractor can be presented by any cryptographic one-way function. Following the notations from [4] the fuzzy extractor is schematically illustrated in figure 3. Here P is the helper data, w is the reference vector, w' is the test vector similar to w in a certain degree and R is the secret key generated from the reference vector w or from the test vector w'.

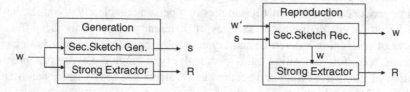

Fig. 3. Fuzzy extractor: generation und reproduction procedures

The secure sketch algorithm alone allows user authentication, but does not guarantee secure preservation of biometric templates.

One of the practical implementation of this idea was given by Vielhauer in [25]. He introduced interval matrix as a helper information and interval mapping procedure as one-way transformation of a fuzzy feature vector to a stable hash vector. In fact, the interval matrix contains feature variances (interval lengths) and zero offset of the first interval for all users individually. The interval mapping comprises the zero offset subtraction and the integer division to the interval length. Thus, this concept can be designated as user-based quantization. Nevertheless, originally it was called biometric hashing. This term will be also used in our work as a general description of the addressed process.

Juels and Wattenberg in [12] suggested error-correcting codes and linear shift of reference vectors to the codeword space for creation of helper data. The process was called "fuzzy commitment scheme". The idea is shown in figure 4. Firstly, the set of

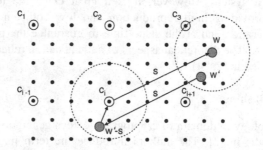

Fig. 4. Codeword mapping in accordance with the fuzzy commitment scheme

codewords $\{c_1, c_2, ..., c_n\}$ is selected based on distribution of biometric data. The helper data s is built as a difference between reference vector w and corresponding codeword c_i. In order to reproduce the codeword c_i from the test vector w', the sketch value s is subtracted and the nearest neighbor in the codeword space is returned. The reference vector w can be reconstructed by addition of s.

In order to show the direct conformity of the fuzzy extractor and the fuzzy commitment scheme, the generation procedure of the fuzzy extractor is given as following, whereby SS corresponds to the *Secure Sketch Generation* procedure, *Ext* is the *Strong Extractor*, *Rec* is the *Reconstruction* procedure and h refers to an arbitrary cryptographic hash function:

Randomly choose i:

$$s = SS(w) = w - c_i$$
$$R = Ext(w) = h(w)$$

The *Reproduction* procedure can be presented as following:

$$R = Ext(Rec(w', s)) = h(Rec(w', s)) = h((\arg\min_k((w'-s), c_k) + s) = h(c_i + s) = h(w)$$

The fuzzy extractor was originally introduced for discrete signals. The feature vectors extracted from biometric data usually contain continuous values. Sutcu et al. in [24] propose practical realization of the secure sketch algorithm, based on fuzzy commitment scheme with double quantization, which is applied to continuous feature vectors. The first quantization with the global quantization step transforms feature data from continuous to integer domain. During the second quantization the integer feature values are mapped to the individual hash values based on user-based quantization step. The difference between hash values and feature values is used as helper data. This scheme was applied to face modality and has shown impressive results regarding the improvement of authentication performance.

Scheidat et al. in [21] adapted the scheme of Sutcu for handwriting features. They compared the authentication as well as hash generation results to the scheme of Vielhauer [25] and figured out that the scheme of Suztu has superior hash generation performance but inferior user authentication performance [21]. This research extends the aforementioned work through the selection of relevant handwriting features in order to enhance the performance of the secure sketch algorithm based on double quantization.

2.2   Feature Selection in Biometrics

Unfortunately, the feature selection problem has been neglected in many biometric studies. Developers probably rely on the ability of a classification algorithm to model user distribution independently from the quality of features. Indeed, some classifiers such as decision trees, adaptive boosting or support vector machine already contain a feature selection mechanism. In literature e.g. [20] this kind of feature selection is called embedded, because of its inherent relation to the classifier. However, the selection of features based on the additional extrinsic analysis can lead to superior results. This was shown e.g. in work of Kira et al. [13]. The authors proposed the Relief algorithm to determine the relevance of each feature for the decision tree relying on instance-based learning. Another example is the FOCUS algorithm of Almuallim et al. [1]. Both algorithms were used together with the ID3 algorithm to induce a decision tree from the training data using only selected features. The resulting classification performance was significantly higher compared to the intrinsic ID3 feature selection, which is based on feature's information gain. In later studies John et al. [11] formally defined the terms relevance and redundancy of features. They originally introduced the division of feature selection approaches to filters and wrappers. One of the main results of their work was the assertion that the feature selection should rely on the relation between features and targets as well as on the classification algorithm [14]. In other words, the wrapper model should be preferred.

The truth is that the feature selection is a general problem of pattern recognition. Comprehensive studies and very detailed surveys can be found [3, 8, 16, 18, 20]. Our investigation relies on the work of Guyon et al. [7]. Both filter and wrapper approaches are studied. For filter-based selection, the feature ranking is done using the correlation coefficient or mutual information. The wrappers are represented by nested subset selection with forward or backward selection or with multiplicative updates and subsequent classification.

Several works bring up a feature selection issue in biometric domain. For instance, Kumar et al. in [15] used the Correlation Based Feature Selection (CFS) swiped from Hall et al. [9] for the bimodal biometric system and investigated the classification performance. In addition, the feature level fusion used in combination with feature selection is studied.

A selection of handwriting features was done in [6]. For feature ranking authors propose the heuristic, which is based on calculation of the scalar Mahalanobis distance between the mean feature value of user's training signatures and the mean feature value of all training signatures. Finally, they suggest 40 features from 100 proposed.

Makrushin et al. in [17] investigated several heuristics-based as well as wrapper-based subset selection approaches and applied them to the biometric hashing algorithm of Vielhauer [25]. Both user authentication and hash generation performances of the algorithm were significantly improved.

3   Secure Sketch Algorithm

The biometric hashing is a concept of the creation of an individual stable value from variable biometric data of a user. This concept is based on the assumption that the intra-class variations of biometric signals are significantly smaller than inter-class variations. Consequently, the variations in user's samples can be reduced through an intelligent quantization or an error-correcting coding. At the same time samples of the different users, which are significantly different, can not be mapped to the same hash value through the quantization, nor properly corrected by error-correcting codes.

However, the error-correcting codes are capable of correcting only a limited number of bits. For instance, the BCH code tolerates errors of up to almost 17% of the component bits [12]. Due to this fact and the high alterability of feature values, it is hard to adapt any standard error-correcting scheme for handwriting features in order to exactly reproduce the reference vectors. Therefore, the smart employment of error-correcting codes leads to sufficient user authentication rates, but reproduction rates remain deficient. Hence, in our experiments, the double quantization algorithm originally proposed in [23] and modified for handwriting features in [21] is used. This scheme seems to be more appropriate for the considered task.

In the description of algorithm the following notations are used: M denotes the number of user, N denotes the number of features, index j defines a particular user, index i refers to a certain feature and f_{ij} is the feature value. The features are considered independently, so that the equations are presented for the fixed index i.

The first quantization with a fixed uniform quantization step transforms continuous feature values to integer format and at the same time strongly reduces the variance of feature values. The global quantization step δ_i is calculated as follows, whereby S_j is the number of trainings samples of user j:

$$\text{var}_{ij} = \max_{k=1,S_j}(f_{ijk}) - \min_{k=1,S_j}(f_{ijk}) \tag{1}$$

$$\delta_i = \max(\min_{j=1,M}(\text{var}_{ij}),1) \tag{2}$$

The value var_{ij} is used to provide the individual quantization step. Firstly, in order to generate the reference value, the average feature value for each user j is calculated:

$$avg_{ij} = 0.5 \cdot \left(\max_{k=1,S_j}(f_{ijk}) + \min_{k=1,S_j}(f_{ijk}) \right) \tag{3}$$

Next, these values are quantized in accordance with global quantization step δ_i, whereby e is the expansion factor of the individual quantization interval σ_{ij}:

$$\sigma_{ij} = \left\lceil \frac{e \cdot \text{var}_{ij}}{\delta_i} \right\rceil \tag{4}$$

$$w_{ij} = \left\lfloor \frac{avg_{ij}}{\delta_i} \right\rfloor \tag{5}$$

By modifying the expansion factor, one can an achieve increase of RR and decrease of CR or vice versa. The expansion factor can be selected for each feature individually. Vector w_j is stored as the user template. The value σ_{ij} is called codebook condition. The scalar codeword c_{ij} is provided by quantization of w_{ij} in accordance with σ_{ij} and back projection to templates space.

$$c_{ij} = round\left(\frac{w_{ij}}{2\sigma_{ij}+1} \right) \cdot (2\sigma_{ij}+1) \tag{6}$$

The helper data (sketch) s is the difference between the quantized average value and the corresponding codeword.

$$s_{ij} = w_{ij} - c_{ij} \qquad (7)$$

Since the sketch s_{ij} is available, the codeword c_{ij} can be reconstructed from any test vector t_j of the user j, which is similar enough to the reference vector avg_j. First, for each feature i, the quantization of the corresponding component of the test vector t_j is done with the global quantization step δ_i:

$$w'_{ij} = \left\lfloor \frac{t_{ij}}{\delta_i} \right\rfloor \qquad (8)$$

Then the sketch is subtracted and the user-based quantization is provided:

$$c'_{ij} = round\left(\frac{w'_{ij} - s_{ij}}{2\sigma_{ij} + 1} \right) \cdot \left(2\sigma_{ij} + 1 \right) \qquad (9)$$

Taking into account that vectors w_j and w'_j are similar to a certain degree, the vectors c_j and c'_j must be equal after this transformation. The template w_j of the user j can be reproduced from the reconstructed codeword by addition of the sketch value.

$$w_{ij} = c'_{ij} + s_{ij} \qquad (10)$$

Finally, the proposed process is illustrated in figure 5.

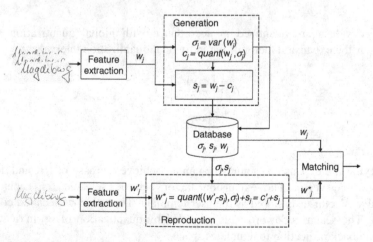

Fig. 5. General scheme of sketch generation and reconstruction processes

How it can be seen in figure 5, no cryptographic hashing of the user's template is provided. In spite of the fact that the strong extractor has to be used in practical applications, the absence of it does not have any influence to the template reconstruction or more precisely to reproduction and collision rates. Indeed, the quantized codeword c_j can be alternatively stored as the user template. This vector cannot be reproduced without an appropriate test sample of the same user and taken alone does not provide any information about w_j. Thus, regarding the definition given in [25] this vector can be designated as the biometric hash vector. The reproduction as well as collision rates in both cases, the reconstruction of the reference vector and the reconstruction of the codeword, are equal.

4   Feature Selection

Kira in [13] gives the following definition of feature selection: "Feature selection is the problem of choosing a small subset of features that ideally is necessary and sufficient to describe the target concept." Regarding this definition, the irrelevant and redundant features should be removed during the feature selection. Therefore a reasonable question arises: "How it could be possible to find out, which features are irrelevant or redundant and what is exactly *relevant* in this scope?" John and Kohavi in [11, 14] give the strict definition of feature relevance. They also define a redundant feature as a feature, which linearly depends on another feature, or on a combination of other features.

A further question to be considered is: "Why are irrelevant or redundant features disturbing for a classification?" Actually, a good classifier should automatically use only useful features and ignore any other ones. Indeed, only a small number of classification schemes comprise embedded feature selection. Kumar et al. in [15] point out some types of negative impact of irrelevant and redundant features to three classification schemes: nearest neighbor rule, naive Bayes classifier and decision trees. Another reason for feature reduction is that the high dimension of feature space leads to classification errors. Experts refer to it as "curse of dimensionality" [5]. Furthermore, the computational resources are always limited and therefore low-dimensional vectors are preferred. Hence, the need of a feature reduction becomes clear.

However, the feature reduction can be done by classic subspace projection methods like principal component analysis [5]. These techniques are beyond the scope of this work, because after the subspace projection the new features do not possess any comprehensible semantic.

4.1   Wrappers vs. Filters

According to the common terminology originally provided by John et al. in [11] the feature selection approaches are divided into wrappers and filters. In order to emphasize the difference, the approaches are schematically illustrated in figure 6.

Wrappers select the feature subset based on particular classifier performance. Hence, the feature selection is inherently connected to the applied classifier. On the one hand, the *optimal feature subset* can be found through the repetition of classification trials with different feature subsets. Optimality is the most notable advantage here. On the other hand, an exhaustive search is required to find out the optimal subset. Given N features there are 2^N feature subsets possible. This exponential relationship between the number of features and the number of possible subsets makes an exhaustive search applicable only for small number of features. Moreover, the single evaluation trial implies the classification of the whole test set and, therefore, the computational complexity depends from the number of test samples as well.

Filters, on the contrary, select the feature subset based on the predefined ranking of features. The ranking is provided based on some quality criterion, which is completely independent of the classification method. Therefore, filters can be considered as a pre-processing step in signal processing workflow. The quality criteria are selected rather intuitively or based on extrinsic expert knowledge. Obviously, until the classification method is known, the feature selection process is never optimal. Anyhow, in particular cases a filter-based feature selection can lead to the optimal feature subset in terms of classification performance. According to Guyon in [7] "Fisher's criterion to rank variables in a classification problem where the covariance matrix is diagonal is optimum for Fisher's linear discriminant classifier". Even though filters do not usually lead to optimal classification performance, they are preferred due to their computational efficiency. Clearly, the quality criterion choice (in other words the appropriate heuristic) is the most critical issue.

In this work several heuristics for filter-based feature selection are evaluated, as well as three editions of wrapper-based feature selection.

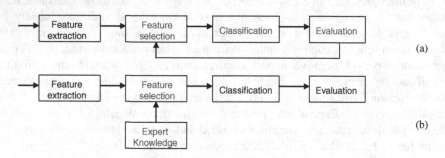

Fig. 6. Comparison of wrappers (a) and filters (b), applied to feature selection

4.2   Exemplary Selected Wrappers

There are several strategies to avoid exhaustive search. In the simplest approach the feature ranking is provided by means of classification with each single feature. Then the best ranked features are included to the target optimal feature subset. Other famous approaches are sequential forward and backward selections (SFS, SBS). The forward selection starts with an empty set and adds the most relevant features one by one at each step. The most relevant feature, in combination with already selected features, has the highest classification error decrease. The iterative process stops when the addition of a new feature does not decrease the classification error. The backward selection starts with the whole feature set and removes the least relevant features one by one at each step. The removal of the least relevant feature leads to the highest classification error decrease (or might even slightly increase it). The iterative process stops when the next removal increases the classification error significantly.

In order to overcome the nesting problem of sequential forward and backward selection, more sophisticated search strategies such as sequential floating forward/backward search [19] or fast branch and bound algorithm [22] can be applied. However, this research is not aimed at comparing all possible approaches. First and foremost, we aim at showing that feature selection can significantly improve the performance of biometric systems and that a time-consuming subset search often has superior results compared to heuristic-based feature ranking.

4.3   Exemplary Selected Filters

In order to avoid the computationally expensive exhaustive search and to be independent from classification algorithm, several heuristics are suggested to define the quality of features. First and foremost, this work aims at proposing quality measures, which reflect the discrimination power of features. The heuristics facilitate the ranking of features through the calculation of quality values. The actual filtering is done by low ranked features cut.

Henceforth some formal notations and terms are provided to avoid any ambiguities and obscurities. The test set of feature vectors x^j with corresponding labels y^j (targets) is given. In biometric context, the labels refer to user identities. The index j refers to the number of test vector. Given that m features are extracted from the raw data, each feature vectors x^j can be then introduced as $x^j = (x_1^j, x_2^j,..., x_m^j)$. Considering all features independently, for each feature i the following notations are used: $x_i = (x_i^1, x_i^2,..., x_i^n)$ is the vector of feature values and $y = (y^1, y^2,..., y^n)$ is the vector of targets, thereby n is the number of vectors in the test set. The aim of the filter is to provide the scalar rank $R(i)$ based on the tuple $\langle x_i, y \rangle$.

ANOVA. Analysis of variance (ANOVA) is a set of statistical models for evaluation of the relationship between within-class scatters and between-class scatter. In order to provide better user discrimination a feature variation σ inside of each user should be as small as possible. Nonetheless, a feature variation between different users should be high. The second value can be defined, for instance, by the difference between mean values μ of users. Equation 11 gives feature quality defined by ANOVA test for the case of two users. Here N_1 and N_2 denote the numbers of test samples of first and second users correspondingly.

$$R(i) = \frac{N_1 \cdot N_2 \cdot (\mu_1 - \mu_2)^2}{N_1 \cdot \sigma_1^2 + N_2 \cdot \sigma_2^2} \tag{11}$$

If more than two users are presented, there are two principal ways to calculate the feature quality (F-value). In the first case, we call it ANOVA-2class, for each user k all other users are considered as only one non-user class and the value F_k can be calculated through the application of equation 11. The final F-value is given by the sum of F_k values.

In the second case the multivariate ANOVA test is applied. The feature variation inside of a user is presented by the sum of deviations of user samples x_{kj} from a user mean value μ_k. The feature variation between different users is presented by the sum of deviations of user mean values μ_k from the global mean value μ. The feature rank (F-value) is given by equation 12. Here K is the number of users and N_k is the number of test samples of the user k.

$$R(i) = \frac{\frac{1}{K-1}\sum_{k=1}^{K} N_k (\mu_k - \mu)^2}{\frac{1}{N-K}\sum_{k=1}^{K}\sum_{j=1}^{N_k} (x_{kj} - \mu_k)^2} \tag{12}$$

Correlation. The use of the correlation between feature values and labels, as the quality criterion of a feature, is described in [7]. Equation 13 provides the Pearson correlation coefficient $R(i)$, whereby the μ_x and μ_y designate mean values of feature i and labels correspondingly.

$$R(i) = \left| \frac{\sum_{x_j}\sum_{y_j}(x_j - \mu_x)(y_j - \mu_y)}{\sqrt{\sum_{x_j}(x_j - \mu_x)^2 \cdot \sum_{y_j}(y_j - \mu_y)^2}} \right| \tag{13}$$

$R(i)$ becomes zero if no correlation between feature and labels is established. This means complete irrelevance of the feature i for user authentication. Contrariwise, $R(i)=1$ designates maximal correlation and therefore absolute relevance of the feature i for the user authentication. It should be noted that the correlation criterion detects only linear dependency between features and labels.

Joint-Entropy. Alternatively, the information theoretic ranking criteria could be used instead of correlation coefficient. The empirical estimation of the mutual information between features and labels gives the quality of the particular feature. Given that the feature values are discrete, the mutual information is given by equation 14.

$$R(i) = \sum_{x_i}\sum_{y} P(X = x_i, Y = y) \cdot \log \frac{P(X = x_i, Y = y)}{P(X = x_i) \cdot P(Y = y)} \tag{14}$$

It is difficult to estimate the real values for the distribution $P(X=x_i)$ of the feature x_i, the prior class probability $P(Y=y)$ and the probability of the joint observation $P(X=x_i, Y=y)$. In case of discrete features, the frequencies calculated from the evaluation data can be used instead.

Entropy-2Class. Another way to build an entropy-based quality criterion relies on the comparison of user and non-user distributions of the particular feature x_i. In case of discrete features the probability distribution can be substituted by the histograms built from the evaluation data. The higher distance between user and non-user histograms designates better discrimination power of the feature. The final quality coefficient is the sum over all users. Four histogram-based distance measures are discussed in this work. These are Kullback-Liebler divergence (KL), Jensen-Shannon distance (JS, also called Jeffrey divergence) and Bhattacharyya distance (Bha). Suppose $H(A) = H_1(A),H_2(A),...,H_N(A)$ is the histogram of feature values from the user A and $H(\bar{A}) = H_1(\bar{A}),H_2(\bar{A}),...,H_N(\bar{A})$ is the histogram of feature values from the remaining users. N is the maximal feature value and K is the number of users. The aforementioned divergences are given by equations 15-17.

Kullback-Liebler:

$$R(i) = \sum_{k=1}^{K} \sum_{j=1}^{N} H_j(k) \cdot \log_2 \left(\frac{H_j(k)}{H_j(\bar{k})} \right) \tag{15}$$

Jensen-Shannon:

$$R(i) = \sum_{k=1}^{K} \sum_{j=1}^{N} \left(H_j(k) \cdot \log_2 \frac{2 \cdot H_j(k)}{H_j(k) + H_j(\bar{k})} + H_j(\bar{k}) \cdot \log_2 \frac{2 \cdot H_j(\bar{k})}{H_j(k) + H_j(\bar{k})} \right) \tag{16}$$

Bhattacharyya:

$$R(i) = \sum_{k=1}^{K} \left(-\ln \sqrt{\sum_{j=1}^{N} H_j(k) \cdot H_j(\bar{k})} \right) \tag{17}$$

Entropy. The same assumption as for the variances in ANOVA could be used for the entropies. The criterion contradistinguishes the inter-class entropy, which is the entropy of the user means $\mu = (\mu_1, \mu_2,...,\mu_k)$ and the intra-class entropy, which is the sum of the entropies of the feature values x_k. The assumption is that for a relevant feature the inter-class entropy is high and intra-class entropy is low. It could be formally given by equation 18. Here N_μ is the maximal value of the user means, N_k is the maximal feature value for user k, whereas K is the number of users.

$$R(i) = \frac{\sum_{j=1}^{N_\mu} H_j(\mu) \cdot \log_2 \frac{1}{H_j(\mu)}}{\sum_{k=1}^{K} \sum_{j=1}^{N_k} H_j(x_k) \cdot \log_2 \frac{1}{H_j(x_k)}} \tag{18}$$

5 Evaluation

The experimental database was collected from 53 donors in laboratory conditions. The tablet PC Toshiba M200 Portege was applied for capturing of handwriting samples. This device is not able to acquire pen altitude and pen azimuth, thus only three signals x(t), y(t) and pressure(t) are exploited to extract the features.

The acquisition was done in three sessions with the interval of at least one month between two sessions in a period of less than 6 months. For each of five written contents, described in the introduction (public PIN, secret PIN, pseudonym, symbol and place), each donor provided 10 instances, which results in a total of 30 instances per user per semantic.

Due to the low number of donors the separation into client and impostor groups was not done. All donors were considered as clients and the experiments were provided in a random attack mode. Any attempt of one client to be verified as another client is interpreted as an impostor trial. In order to be in conformity with a real-life scenario, the samples from the first session were used for enrollment. The samples from the second session were used for the tuning of the verification system and feature selection. The samples from the third session were used for verification test. Regarding the mentioned division of samples the verification test contains 530 genuine trials, corresponding to 53 users times 10 test samples, and 27560 impostor trials, corresponding to 53 users times 52 user claims times 10 test samples.

5.1   Performance Measures

The hash generation scenario implies exact reconstruction of a biometric hash vector. The usual threshold based evaluation used in the user authentication scenario is not appropriate in this case. While a traditional methodology estimates false accept rate (FAR) and false reject rate (FRR) as functions of decision threshold T: FAR(T), FRR(T) the hash generation scenario requires the error estimation in zero point: T=0. In the hash generation scenario the reproduction rate (RR) and collision rate (CR) are used as performance indices [21]. These values are relative sums of identically reproduced hashes in genuine and impostor trials correspondingly. The identical hash reproduction in impostor trial means false acceptance with zero decision threshold and, thus, CR can be denoted as FAR(0). The identical hash reproduction in genuine trial means the correct acceptance with zero decision threshold and, thus, RR can be denoted as 1-FRR(0). Therefore CR and RR have the same nature as FAR and FRR values. In a user authentication scenario the equal error rate (EER) is usually used instead of both curves in order to represent the algorithm performance in an easier way. Similarly, the collision-reproduction rate (CRR) is proposed as a performance index for the hash generation scenario. The CRR is given by equation 19 and can be interpreted as *half total error rate* in zero point HTER(0). In this consideration CR and RR are weighted equally.

$$CRR = \frac{1}{2}(CR + (1 - RR)) \qquad (19)$$

5.2   Expansion Level of Individual Quantization Interval

The selection of expansion factor e, proposed in section 3 is a very important issue for managing the ratio between CR and RR. The selection of a relatively low value of e leads to compact user intervals and therefore to low CR and low RR. On the contrary, the selection of a high value of e leads to very wide user intervals and consequently to high CR and high RR. In marginal cases RR as well as CR is equal to zero or equal to one, resulting in CRR of 0.5. Figure 7 shows the dependency between performance indices and the expansion factor obtained in the tests with 131 features.

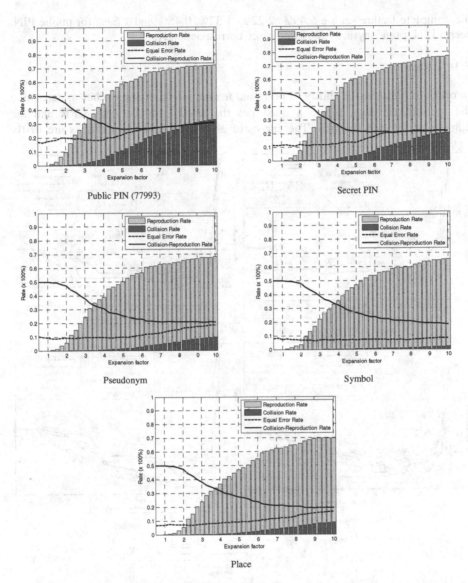

Fig. 7. Dynamics of performance indices (RR, CR, EER, CRR) depending on expansion factor for the complete feature set of 131 features

It is not a good idea to look for the optimal CRR with all 131 features, because it is obvious that with reduction of features RR as well as CR will grow. Since the optimal CRR implies relatively high RR, the RR does not have space to grow. CR at the same time will grow rapidly. Hence, the significant improvement of CRR can not be achieved through feature elimination. We select the expansion factor so that RR is at least 50%. In this case the RR will probably grow faster than CR, so that CRR also grows. The following expansion factors are specified: 4.25 for public PIN and secret PIN, 5 for pseudonym, 5.5 for symbol and place. The corresponding CR values for the complete feature set are 6.49%, 2.22%, 1.32%, 0.45% and 1.69% for public PIN, secret PIN, pseudonym, symbol and place correspondingly.

5.3   Results

In order to illustrate the ability of proposed feature selection approaches to determine the feature relevance, figure 8 illustrates the relationship between CRR and the number of selected features. The curves of all feature selection methods are firstly

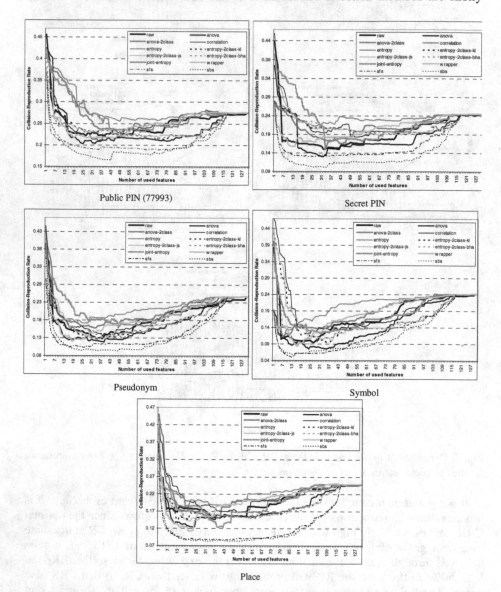

Fig. 8. Collision-Reproduction Rate dynamics depending on feature subset size

falling and afterwards growing. However, global minima are attained in very different positions according to the number of selected features. The black solid curve, called 'raw', is the random ranking of features based on the features' implementation order. There are 13 features without any variance. They do not have any influence on CRR. All feature selection strategies rate these features with zero and therefore put at the end of the ranking list. Thus, the CRR values between 118 and 131 are equal, except the case of a random ranking. It can be clearly seen that not all curves have superior dynamics compared to the raw curve, which means that filter-based feature selection generally does not guarantee an improvement of CRR. However, the global minima of the ANOVA curve are in all cases significantly lower than the global minima of the raw curve. Consequently, it can be asserted that the ANOVA-based feature selection invariably improves the hash generation rates.

Table 2 shows the best results provided by different feature selection methods with a corresponding number of selected features for each semantic class. The first row of the table contains the optimal CRR values, which can be achieved with the complete set of 131 features by modifying the expansion factor of an individual quantization step. Regarding the feature selection methods, these performance values can be considered as reference ones. Table 2 shows that ANOVA is clearly the best heuristic with 20.39%, 12.98%, 11.87%, 7.41% and 12.34% of CRR. Exceptionally, for the place semantic, the joint-entropy heuristic has superior performance, namely 12.29%, which is marginally lower than in the case of ANOVA. It is also interesting to observe that ANOVA has in most cases the better performance than simple wrapper.

The CRR provided by SFS and SBS methods are significantly lower compared to heuristics, even though feature selection and evaluation were provided based on completely different sample sets.

Table 2. The best achieved collision/reproduction rates (in %) with corresponding number of selected features

	public pin (77993)				secret pin				pseudonym				symbol				place			
	RR	CR	CRR	n.feat.	RR	CR	CRR	n.feat.	RR	CR	CRR	n.feat.	RR	CR	CRR	n.feat.	RR	CR	CRR	n.feat.
all features	58.87	10.56	25.85	131	70.38	11.11	20.37	131	67.55	8.58	20.52	131	70.57	5.04	17.24	131	69.43	7.38	18.98	131
raw	76.23	20.53	22.15	39	79.06	9.04	14.99	42	83.59	9.23	12.83	38	90.19	8.92	9.37	27	77.93	8.04	15.06	39
anova	78.68	19.39	20.35	33	83.40	9.32	12.96	31	83.02	6.75	11.87	39	92.64	7.46	7.41	24	89.62	14.30	12.34	23
anova-2class	75.28	19.45	22.08	49	81.70	14.73	16.52	44	77.74	9.22	15.74	34	88.49	11.10	11.30	7	79.25	9.51	15.13	39
correlation	83.59	25.18	20.80	36	80.76	7.32	18.28	53	86.42	13.41	13.50	38	86.23	10.11	11.94	23	72.83	6.19	16.68	52
entropy	62.83	13.96	25.57	49	76.60	19.07	21.23	26	72.64	6.97	17.17	26	86.42	9.11	11.35	8	81.13	17.41	18.14	20
entropy-2class-kl	71.70	14.44	21.37	77	72.64	9.84	18.60	68	85.47	10.89	12.71	35	86.42	5.38	9.48	36	96.04	23.18	13.57	13
entropy-2class-js	71.70	14.74	21.52	74	72.64	9.84	18.60	68	85.28	10.64	12.68	36	85.09	5.24	10.07	39	87.17	15.41	14.12	21
entropy-2class-bha	71.70	14.70	21.50	72	70.19	8.20	19.01	83	81.13	7.38	13.12	52	88.87	6.77	8.95	23	76.42	6.32	14.95	63
joint-entropy	69.81	15.99	23.09	62	82.45	12.54	15.04	33	76.79	8.62	15.91	48	83.02	7.27	12.12	32	87.17	11.74	12.29	39
simple wrapper	73.02	16.28	21.63	32	85.47	16.76	15.64	14	86.42	10.40	11.99	18	89.43	6.06	8.31	17	89.25	11.60	11.18	20
sfs	74.91	12.64	18.87	66	81.70	7.57	12.94	27	86.60	7.07	10.23	26	93.59	3.44	4.93	13	88.30	5.62	8.66	45
sbs	86.42	19.28	16.43	43	90.38	10.45	10.03	34	89.81	8.44	9.32	48	93.77	4.76	5.49	15	91.89	8.32	8.22	33

Comparing the best result from table 2, which is 4.93% CRR (CR 3.44%/RR 93.59%) for the symbol, to the results from [17], in can be noticed that double quantization based biometric hashing has clearly higher performance according to the CRR. In [17], the best CRR, achieved for symbol with 60 features, was 6.32% (CR 6.23%/RR 93.59%).

Table 3. The collision/reproduction rates (in %) obtained with subset of 30 features

	public pin (77993)				secret pin				pseudonym				symbol				place			
	RR	CR	CRR	n.feat.	RR	CR	CRR	n.feat.	RR	CR	CRR	n.feat.	RR	CR	CRR	n.feat.	RR	CR	CRR	n.feat.
all features	58.87	10.56	25.85	131	70.38	11.11	20.37	131	67.55	8.58	20.52	131	70.57	5.04	17.24	131	69.43	7.38	18.98	131
raw	78.30	23.37	22.53	30	82.08	13.93	15.93	30	84.72	12.89	14.08	30	88.11	8.31	10.10	30	80.00	14.76	17.38	30
anova	78.87	20.91	21.02	30	83.40	9.70	13.15	30	83.77	8.16	12.19	30	89.43	5.72	8.14	30	80.00	10.15	15.07	30
anova-2class	79.62	31.26	25.82	30	83.40	19.53	18.06	30	77.93	10.19	16.13	30	74.53	1.84	13.65	30	80.94	12.80	15.93	30
correlation	83.77	26.97	21.60	30	81.51	20.52	19.50	30	87.93	18.07	15.07	30	81.89	8.87	13.49	30	76.60	14.28	18.84	30
entropy	68.87	23.19	27.16	30	73.40	16.29	21.45	30	67.55	5.22	18.84	30	68.11	2.61	17.25	30	68.49	7.89	19.70	30
entropy-2class-ki	76.60	23.04	23.22	30	75.47	17.23	20.88	30	85.66	12.37	13.36	30	86.42	8.87	11.23	30	77.93	11.49	16.78	30
entropy-2class-js	76.60	23.04	23.22	30	75.09	16.43	20.67	30	85.66	12.28	13.31	30	86.79	8.50	10.85	30	78.30	11.49	16.59	30
entropy-2class-bha	77.55	22.95	22.70	30	75.09	16.69	20.80	30	84.91	14.49	14.79	30	85.66	5.74	10.04	30	80.57	12.50	15.97	30
joint-entropy	81.51	35.43	26.96	30	83.96	26.76	21.40	30	87.93	23.22	17.65	30	83.02	7.88	12.43	30	90.00	23.71	16.85	30
simple wrapper	73.02	16.69	21.84	30	70.38	6.57	18.10	30	77.55	6.34	14.40	30	76.79	2.25	12.73	30	75.09	6.06	15.48	30
sfs	77.36	15.61	19.13	30	80.57	7.23	13.33	30	85.85	6.74	10.45	30	89.62	2.02	6.20	30	88.68	6.28	8.80	30
sbs	87.55	22.07	17.26	30	90.57	11.00	10.22	30	90.76	10.07	9.66	30	89.43	2.99	6.78	30	91.89	8.62	8.37	30

The number of features in table 2 was defined a-posteriori for the best CRR obtained from the test. In a real-life scenario the number of features should be defined a-priori as a system parameter. The estimation of the optimal subset size can be done empirically, based on the results of preliminary tests or intuitively. The constant number of used features is also required for adequate generation of a cryptographic key, since the key size depends on the length of the biometric hash vector. In order to illustrate results, which can be obtained in real-life application, the number of features was limited to 30. The corresponding performance values are given in table 3.

Finally, table 4 gives an overview of the most relevant features selected by the best feature selection approach for each semantic class and shows corresponding performance indices: CR, RR, CRR and EER. As it can be seen, the features were selected differently regarding the written content. However, the feature 27 (normalized average velocity in y-direction) is presented in all five subsets. There are several features presented in four subsets. These are 26 (normalized average velocity in x-direction), 67 (ratio between accumulated perimeters of convex hulls around the path segments and the perimeter of the global bounding box), 68 (normalized number of points in left half region), 86 (ratio between the path length and start-end distance), 122 (average pressure in the third points cluster) and 131 (standard deviation of pressure). These features are considered to be invariably relevant. However, the vast majority of features is not presented in optimal subsets. These could be denoted as moderately irrelevant and should be very discreetly used in further works.

Table 4. The subsets of most relevant features

semantic	RR	CR	CRR	EER	FS method	no.feat.	features
public pin (77993)	86,42%	19,28%	16,43%	18,24%	SBS	43	2, 3, 5, 6, 12, 18, 23, 26, 27, 30, 32, 34, 41, 43, 44, 53, 61, 62, 63, 64, 65, 66, 67, 68, 69, 72, 74, 76, 83, 86, 89, 90, 94, 96, 99, 100, 104, 113, 119, 121, 122, 124, 131
secret pin	90,38%	10,45%	10,03%	10,36%	SBS	34	1, 2, 5, 6, 10, 16, 18, 23, 26, 27, 30, 32, 36, 38, 39, 40, 54, 60, 61, 65, 67, 68, 70, 76, 81, 85, 86, 89, 97, 104, 113, 122, 125, 131
pseudonym	89,81%	8,44%	9,32%	9,61%	SBS	48	3, 8, 14, 16, 17, 18, 26, 27, 31, 33, 34, 35, 37, 41, 44, 49, 51, 52, 53, 55, 56, 59, 61, 64, 66, 67, 68, 69, 72, 73, 74, 76, 87, 91, 94, 95, 96, 97, 98, 99, 105, 107, 111, 118, 121, 122, 125, 131
symbol	93,59%	3,44%	4,93%	5,53%	SFS	13	4, 6, 26, 27, 49, 50, 52, 54, 55, 78, 80, 82, 86
place	91,89%	8,32%	8,22%	8,30%	SBS	33	3, 5, 13, 27, 30, 35, 36, 39, 42, 44, 46, 51, 59, 60, 63, 67, 68, 69, 71, 73, 74, 79, 82, 83, 86, 87, 89, 91, 95, 97, 122, 123, 131

6   Conclusion and Further Work

The experimental results shown that the reduction of the feature set by elimination of less relevant features significantly improves the hash generation performance of the considered secure sketch based biometric system.

The filter-based and wrapper-based approaches to feature selection were investigated and several examples of both were experimentally evaluated on handwriting features. It has been shown that filter-based feature selection does not guarantee the improvement of collision/reproduction rates, even though it can be very useful in some cases. Indeed, the ANOVA test is identified as the best heuristic and often demonstrates better performance than ranking based on the classification with each single feature. The greedy search approaches such as sequential forward or backward search invariably lead to improvement of collision/reproduction rates and generally show better results than filters. However, the wrapper-based feature subset selection is a time-consuming process, even if an exhaustive search is not carried out. Furthermore, wrappers are intrinsically associated with classifier performance. Thus, the selected feature subset should not be necessarily an optimal one for another classifier. Consequently, once the classifier is known and the test set is given, wrappers are preferable in any other cases we suggest to use ANOVA test for feature selection.

It is rather difficult to point out features, which are universally suitable for all written contents. The optimal subsets for each semantic is presented individually and seven features (normalized average velocity in x/y-direction, ratio between accumulated perimeters of convex hulls around the path segments and the perimeter of the global bounding box, normalized number of points in left half region, ratio between the path length and start-end distance, average pressure in the third points cluster and standard deviation of pressure) are specified as suitable independently from written content.

Before feature selection, the most appropriate handwriting content (symbol) has a CR of 5.04% and a RR of 70.57%. After sequential forward selection the optimal subset of 13 features is found. The CR is reduced to 3.44% and the RR is increased to 93.59%.

Future research will be dedicated to more sophisticated wrapper approaches such as sequential floating forward/backward search and branch and bound algorithm. Furthermore, we have been continuously working on enlargement of our handwriting database and development of evaluation protocols. The further crucial issue to be investigated is the hash entropy and security analysis of the resulting biometric system.

Acknowledgement. This work is partly supported by the Deutsche Forschungsgemeinschaft (DFG, German Research Foundation) in framework of the project "Writing Print". Our special thanks go to Prof. Jana Dittmann for fruitful discussions on biometric hashing and cryptography.

References

1. Almuallim, H., Dietterich, T.G.: Learning With Many Irrelevant Features. In: Proc. of the Ninth National Conference on Artificial Intelligence, pp. 547–552 (1991)
2. Balakirsky, V.B., Han Vinckin, A.J.: Biometric Authentication Based on Significant Parameters. In: Vielhauer, C., Dittmann, J., Drygajlo, A., Juul, N.C., Fairhurst, M.C. (eds.) BioID 2011. LNCS, vol. 6583, pp. 13–24. Springer, Heidelberg (2011)
3. Dash, M., Liu, H.: Feature selection for classification. Journal of Intelligent Data Analysis 1(1-4), 131–156 (1997)
4. Dodis, Y., Ostrovsky, R., Reyzin, L., Smith, A.: Fuzzy Extractors: How to Generate Strong Keys from Biometrics and Other Noisy Data. SIAM J. Comput. 38(1), 97–139 (2008)
5. Duda, R.O., Hart, P.E., Stork, D.G.: Pattern Classification, 2nd edn. Wiley-Interscience (2000)
6. Fiérrez-Aguilar, J., Nanni, L., Lopez-Peñalba, J., Ortega-Garcia, J., Maltoni, D.: An On-Line Signature Verification System Based on Fusion of Local and Global Information. In: Kanade, T., Jain, A., Ratha, N.K. (eds.) AVBPA 2005. LNCS, vol. 3546, pp. 523–532. Springer, Heidelberg (2005)
7. Guyon, I., Elisseeff, A.: An Introduction to Variable and Feature Selection. Journal of Machine Learning Research 3, 1157–1182 (2003)
8. Guyon, I., Gunn, S., Nikravesh, M., Zadeh, L.: Feature Extraction, Foundations and Applications. STUDFUZZ. Physica-Verlag, Springer (2006)
9. Hall, M.A., Smith, L.A.: Practical feature subset selection for machine learning. In: Proc. of the 21st Australian Computer Science Conference, pp. 181–191 (1998)
10. Jain, A.K., Nandakumar, K., Nagar, A.: Biometric Template Security. EURASIP Journal on Advances in Signal Processing, Article ID 579416 (2008)
11. John, G.H., Kohavi, R., Pfleger, K.: Irrelevant Features and the Subset Selection Problem. In: Proc. of the International Conference on Machine Learning, pp. 121–129 (1994)
12. Juels A., Wattenberg, M.: A Fuzzy Commitment Scheme. In: Proc. of the ACM Conference on Computer and Communications Security, pp. 28–36 (1999)
13. Kira, K., Rendell, L.A.: The feature selection problem: Traditional methods and a new algorithm. In: Proc. 10th National Conference on Artificial Intelligence, pp. 129–134 (1992)
14. Kohavi, R., John, G.H.: Wrappers for Feature Subset Selection. Journal of Artificial Intelligence 97(1), 273–324 (1997)
15. Kumar, A., Zhang, D.: Biometric Recognition Using Feature Selection and Combination. In: Kanade, T., Jain, A., Ratha, N.K. (eds.) AVBPA 2005. LNCS, vol. 3546, pp. 813–822. Springer, Heidelberg (2005)
16. Liu, H., Motoda, H. (eds.): Computational Methods of Feature Selection. Data Mining and Knowledge Discovery Series. Chapman & Hall/ CRC, Taylor & Francis Group, LLC (2008)
17. Makrushin, A., Scheidat, T., Vielhauer, C.: Handwriting Biometrics: Feature Selection Based Improvements in Authentication and Hash Generation Accuracy. In: Vielhauer, C., Dittmann, J., Drygajlo, A., Juul, N.C., Fairhurst, M.C. (eds.) BioID 2011. LNCS, vol. 6583, pp. 37–48. Springer, Heidelberg (2011)
18. Molina, L.C., Belanche, L., Nebot, A.: Feature Selection Algorithms: A survey and experimental evaluation. In: Proc. IEEE Int. Conf. on Data Mining, pp. 306–313 (2002)
19. Pudil, P., Novovicová, J., Kittler, J.: Floating search methods in feature selection. Pattern Recognition Letters 15(11), 1119–1125 (1994)

20. Saeys, Y., Inza, I., Larrañaga, P.: A review of feature selection techniques in bioinformatics. Bioinformatics 23(19), 2507–2517 (2007)
21. Scheidat, T., Vielhauer, C., Dittmann, J.: Biometric hash generation and user authentication based on handwriting using secure sketches. In: Proc. ISPA 2009, pp. 550–555 (2009)
22. Somol, P., Pudil, P., Kittler, J.: Fast Branch & Bound Algorithms For Optimal Feature Selection. IEEE Transactions on Pattern Analysis and Machine Intelligence 26(7), 900–912 (2004)
23. Sutcu, Y., Li, Q., Memon, N.: Protecting Biometric Templates with Sketch: Theory and Practice. IEEE Trans. on Information Forensics and Security 2(3), 503–512 (2007)
24. Verbitskiy, E., Tuyls, P., Denteneer, D., Linnartz, J.-P.: Reliable biometric authentication with privacy protection. In: Proc. 24th Benelux Symposium on Information Theory, pp. 125–132 (2003)
25. Vielhauer, C.: Biometric User Authentication for IT Security: From Fundamentals to Handwriting. Springer (2006)

Feature-Based Forensic Camera Model Identification

Thomas Gloe

Technische Universität Dresden,
Institute of Systems Architecture,
01062 Dresden, Germany
Thomas.Gloe@tu-dresden.de

Abstract. State-of-the-art digital forensic techniques for camera model identification draw attention on different sets of features to assign an image to the employed source model. This paper complements existing work, by a comprehensive evaluation of known feature sets employing a large set of 26 camera models with altogether 74 devices. We achieved the highest accuracies using the extended colour feature set and present several detail experiments to validate the ability of the features to separate between camera models and not between devices. Analysing more than 16,000 images, we present a comprehensive evaluation on 1) the number of required images and devices for training, 2) the influence of the number of camera models and camera settings on the detection results and 3) possibilities to handle unknown camera models when not all models coming into question are available or are even known. All experiments in this paper suggest: feature-based forensic camera model identification works in practice and provides reliable results even if only one device for each camera model under investigation is available to the forensic investigator.

1 Introduction

The abundance of digital photographs in everyday life and the trust placed into them as pieces of evidence raises a need for reliable forensic techniques to test the authenticity of digital images. The increasing number of available techniques can be broadly divided into image source identification and manipulation detection [1]. This paper concentrates on the former, and, more specifically, on camera *model* identification. Camera model identification is relevant in practice if the forensic investigator ...

- knows that a given image has been taken with a digital camera (otherwise she would use a scheme targeted to distinguish between *types* of acquisition devices, e.g., scanner, digital camera, or computer-generated [2,3]),
- but does not have a set of independent images unequivocally shot with exactly the same *device* as the suspect image (otherwise she would use a method for camera *device* identification based on the intrinsic fingerprint embedded in each sensors' pattern noise [4,5,6,7,8]).

Y.Q. Shi (Ed.): Transactions on DHMS VIII, LNCS 7228, pp. 42–62, 2012.

Forensic investigators typically have to find answers to the following questions related to camera model identification: "which camera model was (most likely) used to shoot this given image?", for the identification scenario; or, if prior beliefs prevail, "has this image been shot with a Canon Ixus 70 camera?", for the validation scenario.

Techniques trying to answer these questions require characteristics covering differences between camera models, while occurring very similar between devices of one model. Common ingredients are depicted in Fig. 1 in the simplified acquisition pipeline of a digital camera. For example, aberrations introduced by the lens, are specific to models sharing the same optical system, e.g. [9,10]. Estimating the configuration of the colour filter array (CFA) or determining the employed method for colour interpolation allows a basic discrimination between groups of camera models, e.g. [11,12]. Furthermore, compression parameters [13], meta data [14] and the employed file structure can help to isolate questionable models.

This paper belongs to feature-based camera model identification based on characteristics covering coarse noise properties, colour reproduction and image quality. This approach has been first proposed by Kharrazi, Sencar and Memon [15] for the identification of digital camera models and was further investigated by Çeliktutan, Avcibas and Sankur for low resolution mobile-phone cameras [16,17]. Using small sets of digital cameras or mobile-phone cameras, reliable results for both camera and mobile-phone model identification were reported.

In our previous work [18], we started to explore the influence of the cardinality and between-model variance of the training set on the overall classification performance employing a subset of 12 camera models of the 'Dresden Image Database' [19]. The reported results with average success rates above 90% are promising and indicate the possibility to apply this scheme in practice. However, the scalability in scenarios with even more camera models, the influence of the different sets of features [15,17,18] as well as the handling of unknown camera models require further attention.

Based on all natural images in the 'Dresden Image Database' including 26 camera models with altogether 74 devices, we compare different sets of features and investigate the influence of feature selection under practical relevant conditions. We extend our previous analysis in [18] on the determined best feature set and evaluate the ability to separate between different models and not between different devices. A discussion on the influence of the number of images, devices and camera models on the detection results gives valuable clues for creating appropriate training data sets. Finally, we draw attention to handle unknown cameras in open sets of camera models and deepen our investigations presented at DAGM 2011 [20]. We believe that this paper contains valuable information for forensic investigators with typically limited resource and limited budgets to correctly train a feature-based forensic camera model identification scheme.

The remainder of the paper is organised as follows: Section 2 introduces the general scheme for camera model identification and discusses the different feature sets. Section 3 describes the employed data set and basic test settings used in our

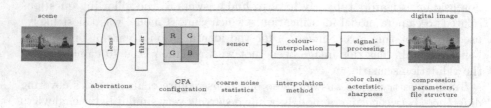

Fig. 1. Simplified image acquisition pipeline of a digital camera and possible sources of model-dependent characteristics

investigations. An detailed analysis of feature-based camera model identification employing closed model sets, where all questioned camera models are considered known, is presented in Sec. 4. Section 5 considers the problem of unknown camera models and possible false accusation in so called open sets. Finally, the paper concludes with a discussion in Sec. 6.

2   Camera Model Identification

Feature-based forensic camera model identification is motivated by differences in the internal image acquisition pipeline of digital camera models [15]. To create visually pleasant images, the manufacturers specifically fine-tune the components and algorithms for each digital camera model. Details on this fine-tuning are usually considered trade secrets. Nevertheless we can capture some variation with specific features. These features are required to be stable for all devices of one model to capture characteristics inherent in each image acquired with the same model. For instance, we can try to characterise the camera model-dependent combination of colour filter array and colour interpolation algorithm, or the algorithms implemented in the internal signal processing pipeline including, for example, the white-point correction.

The first step in feature-based forensic camera model identification is the estimation of a set of features in images taken with all camera models coming into question. Employing the estimated features, second, a machine learning algorithm can be trained to, third, determine or to validate the probable source of an image. In literature, a support vector machine (SVM) is used for machine learning and the major difference between previously proposed schemes relies in the set of employed features. The features are broadly classified into four main groups: Colour characteristics ($\mathcal{F}_{col}$) [15] describing the colour reproduction of a camera model, wavelet statistics ($\mathcal{F}_{wav}$) [21] coarsely quantifying noise, image quality metrics ($\mathcal{F}_{iqm}$) [22] measuring noise and sharpness (quality of scene reproduction by the optical system), and binary similarity measures ($\mathcal{F}_{bsm}$) [23] characterising relations between different bit planes of one colour channel as well as between different colour channels.

Kharrazi, Sencar, and Memon introduced feature-based camera model identification employing a set of 34 features $\mathcal{F}_{Khar}$ including $\mathcal{F}_{col}$, $\mathcal{F}_{iqm}$ and $\mathcal{F}_{wav}$ [15].

Another set of features $\mathcal{F}_{\text{Çeli}}$ was proposed by Çeliktutan et al. [17] containing a similar group of wavelet statistics $\mathcal{F}_{\text{wav}}$ and image quality metrics $\mathcal{F}_{\text{iqm}}$, complemented with binary similarity measures $\mathcal{F}_{\text{bsm}}$. Contrary to Kharrazi et al., $\mathcal{F}_{\text{iqm}}$ are analysed for each colour channel separately and an extended set of $\mathcal{F}_{\text{wav}}$ is calculated for up to 4 wavelet sub bands. Altogether, the feature set consists of 592 characteristics.

In our earlier work [18], we used an *extended* version $\mathcal{F}_{\text{ext}}$ of the original Kharrazi et al. feature set, consisting of 46 features. We added some new colour features and, motivated by the work of Farid and Lyu [21] as well as Çeliktutan et al., calculated an extended set of wavelet features. Furthermore, we investigated the combination of the 46 features with characteristics of lateral chromatic aberration [10,20] with little success. Lateral chromatic aberration as well as aberrations in general are dependent on focal length and focus settings. The resulting variance makes it very difficult to generate a comprehensive measurement of all possible settings necessary for reliable feature-based camera model identification.

Additionally to the three mentioned feature sets, within this paper, we investigate an *extended colour* feature set $\mathcal{F}_{\text{extc}}$, including the features of our extended set for each colour channel separately (82 features), and a *complete* feature set $\mathcal{F}_{\text{comp}}$ joining all features of the four basic feature groups: $\mathcal{F}_{\text{col}}$, $\mathcal{F}_{\text{wav}}$, $\mathcal{F}_{\text{iqm}}$ and $\mathcal{F}_{\text{bsm}}$.

3   Test Setup

A key factor in designing and evaluating techniques for camera model identification is in the composition of a suitable benchmark database. To assure that arbitrary features capture characteristics of the model rather than of the device or image contents, a database of images with comparable contents shot with multiple models and *multiple devices per model* is required. Only recently, we compiled the 'Dresden Image Database' for this very purpose [19].

Table 1 lists the 26 employed camera models, the number of corresponding devices and images, as well as basic camera specifications. The database includes both, typical consumer digital camera models and semi-professional digital SLR cameras. In some investigations the computational complexity was quite demanding and a reduced set of camera models similar to our previous work was employed [18]. We abbreviate the complete and reduced sets of camera models with symbols $\mathcal{M}_{\text{all}}$ and $\mathcal{M}_{\text{red}}$.

To provide images with similar content, all images in the database are created employing a specific image acquisition procedure. A tripod was fixed for each motif and using each device three or more scenes have been taken with different focal length settings. For logistical reasons all camera models were split into set A and B, both covering different motifs (cf. [19] for a more detailed description). Identifiers of the employed model, device id, camera settings and the acquired motif are stored together with each image and enable to analyse features under selected constraints.

Altogether, 16,958 original images stored in the JPEG format at full resolution were analysed. Compared to previous work, where a small set of digital cameras (5 camera models) [15] or a small set of low resolution mobile-phone cameras (13 mobile-phone models with altogether 16 devices) [17] was investigated, the employed data set allows the evaluation of feature-based camera model identification under comprehensive settings. Another difference is the variation in focal length and flash settings.

Analysing feature-based camera model identification requires a set $\mathcal{I}_{\text{train}} \subset \mathcal{I}$ of images to *train* and a set $\mathcal{I}_{\text{test}}$ of images to optimise the detection performance of the employed machine learning algorithm. An independent *validation* set $\mathcal{I}_{\text{val}}$ is required to report practical relevant detection results. In real scenarios, we expect different devices employed for acquiring the image under investigation and the images available for machine learning. Consequently, we partition the set of available devices $\mathcal{D}^{(m)}$ of each camera model m in a set of devices for machine learning $\mathcal{D}^{(m)}_{\text{train,test}}$ and a disjoint set of devices for validating the detection results $\mathcal{D}^{(m)}_{\text{val}} = \mathcal{D}^{(m)}/\mathcal{D}^{(m)}_{\text{train,test}}$. The expected difference of image content between images available during machine learning and images provided for classification makes a reasonable separation of the set of available motifs $\mathcal{P}$ necessary. To report detection results independently of the image content, requires images of the same motifs for each device. Ideally, a large number of different motifs for training, testing and validating feature-based camera model identification exists. However, due to the limited number of images in our database, we decided to separate $\mathcal{P}$ in a set of training $\mathcal{P}_{\text{train}}$ and a disjoint set of test and validation $\mathcal{P}_{\text{test,val}}$ motifs. The stored device (d) and motif (p) identifiers enable the assignment of each image $i \in \mathcal{I}$ to its corresponding set:

$$\mathcal{I}_{\text{train}} = \{i | d_i \in \mathcal{D}_{\text{train,test}} \wedge p_i \in \mathcal{P}_{\text{train}}\} \tag{1}$$

$$\mathcal{I}_{\text{test}} = \{i | d_i \in \mathcal{D}_{\text{train,test}} \wedge p_i \in \mathcal{P}_{\text{test,val}}\} \tag{2}$$

$$\mathcal{I}_{\text{val}} = \{i | d_i \in \mathcal{D}_{\text{val}} \wedge p_i \in \mathcal{P}_{\text{test,val}}\} \tag{3}$$

Experimental results in this paper are based on cross-validation using a fixed set of 100 different partitionings of $\mathcal{I}$ unless otherwise stated. We assigned devices and motifs to the corresponding training, test and validation sets randomly with preset cardinalities ($|\mathcal{D}^{(m)}_{\text{train,test}}| = 1$, $|\mathcal{P}_{\text{train}}| = 26$). All available camera models are included to make the identification task challenging and realistic. For some camera models only 1 device is available (e.g., models of make Agfa) and detection results are only computed for the test images. The fixed partitionings make the experiments repeatable and we present average results balancing between best and worst results.

Besides the public available set of images in the 'Dresden Image Database', we employed an additional set of snapshot images created only for some selected camera models. These images form another validation set with scene content and camera settings independent to the structured design of the official database. Due to the lack of a tripod during image acquisition, the quality is not always convincing and also blurred images are included.

All investigations in this paper make use of a support vector machine implementation developed by Chang and Lin with a radial based kernel function [24] provided through the interface of the R package e1071. More precisely, we employed the multi-class classification scheme of LIBSVM to separate between different camera models. The implementation of the library solves the multi-class problem by creating single binary SVMs for all pairs of different classes (one-versus-one) and a voting scheme determines the most probable class.

Table 1. List of digital camera models included in this study; number of devices per model, basic camera specifications and number of available images. (*) indicates models included in the reduced set $\mathcal{M}_{red}$ necessary to investigate the large feature sets ($\mathcal{F}_{\text{Çeli}}, \mathcal{F}_{comp}$).

make	model	no. devices	resolution [pixel]	sensor size [inch or mm]	focal length [mm]	no. images (flash released) set A	set B	Σ	snapshots
Agfa	DC-504	1	4032×3024	-	7.1	78 (14)	91 (10)	169 (24)	
Agfa	DC-733s	1	3072×2304	-	6.2–18.6	150 (21)	128 (3)	278 (24)	
Agfa	DC-830i	1	3264×2448	-	6.2–18.6	176 (50)	187 (31)	363 (81)	
Agfa	Sensor505-X	1	2592×1944	-	7.5	87 (11)	85 (9)	172 (20)	
Agfa	Sensor530s	1	4032×3024	-	6.1–18.3	195 (50)	177 (35)	372 (85)	
Canon	Ixus55	1	2592×1944	1/2.5"	5.8–17.4	224 (52)		224 (52)	
Canon	Ixus70 (*)	3	3072×2304	1/2.5"	5.8–17.4	567 (119)		567 (119)	
Canon	PowerShot A640	1	3648×2736	1/1.8"	7.3–29.2		188 (23)	188 (23)	
Casio	EX-Z150 (*)	5	3264×2448	1/2.5"	4.65–18.6	924 (178)		924 (178)	
FujiFilm	FinePix J50	3	3264×2448	1/2.5"	6.2–31.0		630 (99)	630 (99)	503 (210)
Kodak	M1063 (*)	5	2748×3664	1/2.33"	5.7–17.1	1070 (330)	1321 (289)	2391 (619)	
Nikon	CoolPix S710 (*)	5	4352×3264	1/1.72"	6.0–21.6	925 (173)		925 (173)	
Nikon	D200 (*)	2	3872×2592	23.6×15.8 mm	18 – 135/17 – 55	752 (79)		752 (79)	
Nikon	D70/D70s	2/2	3008×2000	23.7×15.6 mm	18–200	736 (78)		736 (78)	
Olympus	μ1050SW (*)	5	3648×2736	1/2.33"	6.7–20.1	1040 (342)		1040 (342)	
Panasonic	DMC-FZ50	3	3648×2736	1/1.8"	7.4–88.8		931 (115)	931 (115)	832 (426)
Pentax	Optio A40	4	4000×3000	1/1.7"	7.9–23.7		638 (90)	638 (90)	574 (445)
Pentax	Optio W60	1	3648×2736	1/2.3"	5.0–25.0		192 (23)	192 (23)	308 (290)
Praktica	DCZ5.9 (*)	5	2560×1920	1/2.5"	5.4–16.2	1019 (273)		1019 (273)	
Ricoh	GX100	5	3648×2736	1/1.75"	5.1–15.3		854 (112)	854 (112)	1794 (1106)
Rollei	RCP-7325XS (*)	3	3072×2304	1/2.5"	5.8–17.4	589 (148)		589 (148)	
Samsung	L74wide (*)	3	3072×2304	1/2.5"	4.7–16.7	686 (144)		686 (144)	
Samsung	NV15 (*)	3	3648×2736	1/1.8"	7.3–21.9	645 (110)		645 (110)	
Sony	DSC-H50	2	3456×2592	1/2.3"	5.2–78.0		541 (57)	541 (57)	375 (45)
Sony	DSC-T77	4	3648×2736	1/2.3"	6.18–24.7		725 (88)	725 (88)	863 (346)
Sony	DSC-W170	2	3648×2736	1/2.3"	5.0–25.0		405 (52)	405 (52)	244 (38)
Σ		74				9863 (2172)	7093 (1036)	16956 (3208)	5493 (2906)

4 Camera-Model Identification in Closed Sets

In the first part of our investigations, we assume that all camera models coming into question are known. We call sets including only known camera models *closed sets*. In practice, it might be difficult to consider all possibly employed camera models during image acquisition and unknown camera models might cause false accusations. This problem is an inherent property of multi-class SVMs, which always assign a sample to one of the trained classes. We discuss this problem in Sec. 5 and present first solutions to cover unknown models in *open sets*.

4.1 Benchmarking Feature Sets

Before we will take a closer look at the ability of the features to separate between different camera models and not between different devices, we will first analyse the performance of the five feature sets described in Sec. 2.

Therefore, we optimised the basic parameters of a SVM with a radial based kernel function using grid-search with γ in the range of $2^{3,2,\ldots,-15}$ and C in the range of $2^{-5,-4,\ldots,15}$. The optimisation was done separately for each of the fixed 100 partitionings to report average and standard deviation of the accuracies (i.e., the average detection rate over all camera models) under optimal parameter settings in Tab. 2. The required computational time increased exceptionally when we tried to optimise a SVM for $\mathcal{M}_{\text{all}}$ in combination with the large feature sets ($\mathcal{F}_{\text{Çeli}}, \mathcal{F}_{\text{comp}}$) and we decided to calculate the results only for $\mathcal{M}_{\text{red}}$.

Table 2. Average accuracies for five different feature sets over 100 fixed partitionings (standard deviation is enclosed in brackets). Best accuracies are in bold for $\mathcal{M}_{\text{all}}, \mathcal{M}_{\text{red}}$ in combination with $\mathcal{I}_{\text{test}}, \mathcal{I}_{\text{val}}$.

	model set	feature set				
		$\mathcal{F}_{\text{Khar}}$	$\mathcal{F}_{\text{ext}}$	$\mathcal{F}_{\text{extc}}$	$\mathcal{F}_{\text{Çeli}}$	$\mathcal{F}_{\text{comp}}$
test data $\mathcal{I}_{\text{test}}$	$\mathcal{M}_{\text{red}}$ ($w_{\text{Khar,grey}}$)	95.62% (1.60)	97.45% (1.27)	97.94% (1.10)	94.07% (1.61)	94.00% (1.61)
	$\mathcal{M}_{\text{red}}$ ($w_{\text{Khar,col}}$)	-	-	**98.06%** (1.02)	95.32% (1.55)	95.30% (1.49)
	$\mathcal{M}_{\text{red}}$ ($w_{\text{DB8,grey}}$)	95.57% (1.60)	97.13% (1.34)	97.73% (1.18)	94.29% (1.45)	94.29% (1.42)
	$\mathcal{M}_{\text{red}}$ ($w_{\text{DB8,col}}$)	-	-	97.83% (1.03)	95.23% (1.27)	95.24% (1.26)
	$\mathcal{M}_{\text{all}}$ ($w_{\text{Khar,grey}}$)	89.29% (2.46)	91.69% (2.33)	92.71% (2.25)	-	-
	$\mathcal{M}_{\text{all}}$ ($w_{\text{Khar,col}}$)	-	-	93.08% (1.95)	-	-
	$\mathcal{M}_{\text{all}}$ ($w_{\text{DB8,grey}}$)	89.26% (2.51)	91.51% (2.32)	92.85% (2.20)	-	-
	$\mathcal{M}_{\text{all}}$ ($w_{\text{DB8,col}}$)	-	-	**93.12%** (1.94)	-	-
validation data $\mathcal{I}_{\text{val}}$	$\mathcal{M}_{\text{red}}$ ($w_{\text{Khar,grey}}$)	93.14% (1.93)	95.27% (1.70)	96.12% (1.49)	91.50% (1.79)	91.47% (1.76)
	$\mathcal{M}_{\text{red}}$ ($w_{\text{Khar,col}}$)	-	-	**96.36%** (1.32)	92.80% (1.66)	92.70% (1.67)
	$\mathcal{M}_{\text{red}}$ ($w_{\text{DB8,grey}}$)	93.18% (1.94)	94.96% (1.80)	96.01% (1.56)	92.66% (1.73)	92.65% (1.74)
	$\mathcal{M}_{\text{red}}$ ($w_{\text{DB8,col}}$)	-	-	96.18% (1.40)	93.75% (1.58)	93.69% (1.63)
	$\mathcal{M}_{\text{all}}$ ($w_{\text{Khar,grey}}$)	85.62% (2.94)	88.60% (2.87)	89.98% (2.63)	-	-
	$\mathcal{M}_{\text{all}}$ ($w_{\text{Khar,col}}$)	-	-	90.67% (2.42)	-	-
	$\mathcal{M}_{\text{all}}$ ($w_{\text{DB8,grey}}$)	85.79% (2.86)	88.70% (2.85)	90.41% (2.59)	-	-
	$\mathcal{M}_{\text{all}}$ ($w_{\text{DB8,col}}$)	-	-	**90.93%** (2.48)	-	-

We also experimented with the influence of the selected wavelet filter to calculate the wavelet statistics. Namely, we tested a wavelet filter originally employed by Kharrazi et al. (w_{Khar}) and a Daubechies 8 filter (w_{DB8}) commonly used for the estimation of sensor noise [4]. For the feature sets $\mathcal{F}_{\text{extc}}$, $\mathcal{F}_{\text{Çeli}}$ and $\mathcal{F}_{\text{comp}}$, we included also tests with and without averaging the wavelet statistics of each colour channel (w_{grey}, w_{col}).

It can be expected, that increasing the number of known camera models increases also the chance, that different models share similar characteristics. The decrease of accuracy in case of $\mathcal{M}_{\text{all}}$ compared to $\mathcal{M}_{\text{red}}$ demonstrates this effect and might result in less accurate decisions when using sets with considerably more than 26 models. Furthermore, the results employing $\mathcal{I}_{\text{test}}$ (images acquired with the same device as the training data) are always better than the results for $\mathcal{I}_{\text{val}}$ (images acquired with other devices). This indicates small variations in the analysed characteristics between devices of one model.

We obtained the best results in this scenario employing $\mathcal{F}_{\text{extc}}$ for both sets of camera models $\mathcal{M}_{\text{all}}$ and $\mathcal{M}_{\text{red}}$. Differences in the results related to the two employed wavelet filters are negligible and depend on the employed feature set. In contrast, using the wavelet statistics for each colour channel separately, increases the accuracy slightly in all cases. Contrary to our expectations, adding binary similarity measures $\mathcal{F}_{bsm}$ did not increase the identification performance for camera models available in the 'Dresden Image Database'. In fact, the larger number of features seem to complicate the training of the SVM. Çeliktutan et al. therefore applied feature selection to reduce the number of features and to increase the identification performance.

4.2 Feature Selection

Based on the previous tests, we decided to try feature selection to investigate the possibility to improve the accuracy. We employed sequential forward floating search (SFFS) [25] on $\mathcal{F}_{extc}$ and $\mathcal{F}_{comp}$. Features in $\mathcal{F}_{extc}$ were analysed using $\mathcal{M}_{red}$ and $\mathcal{M}_{all}$ and, again due to the computational constraints, $\mathcal{F}_{comp}$ was tested only with $\mathcal{M}_{red}$ resulting in altogether three test configurations. Furthermore, we restricted all following experiments to wavelet statistics based on $w_{DB8,col}$. Knowing that the selection of motifs and devices employed for training might influence feature selection, we applied SFFS to the first 10 of the 100 fixed partitionings of $\mathcal{I}$.

Figure 2 depicts the relation between accuracy and number of selected features for two partitionings with the best and worst achieved maximum accuracy for $\mathcal{I}_{test}$. In this example, we used $\mathcal{F}_{extc}$ together with $\mathcal{M}_{red}$ and it was possible to obtain an accuracy above 98% for $\mathcal{I}_{test}$ for all 10 partitionings of $\mathcal{I}$. In contrast, the results for $\mathcal{I}_{val}$ are worse and are only above 98% in the best case.

SFFS tries to select features according to their importance on the overall classification accuracy and we would expect a similar order of selected features

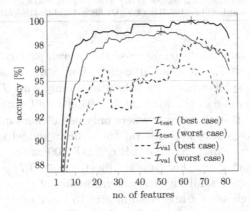

Fig. 2. Number of selected features of $\mathcal{F}_{extc}$ in relation to the achieved accuracy using $\mathcal{M}_{red}$. 2 partitionings with the best and worst accuracy for $\mathcal{I}_{test}$ after feature selection are depicted (both above 98%). Symbols + mark the highest accuracy obtained in both cases.

for all 10 partitionings depending on the employed feature set. While there are indeed some features always in the range of the first 30 most important features, the concrete partitioning of devices and motifs employed for training made the ordering of most features more variable than expected. Considering the worst case in Fig. 2, the increase in accuracy is not always continuous and makes the selection of an universal set of features even more difficult.

Therefore, we used all 30 sets of the best selected features (3 test configurations × 10 partitionings of $\mathcal{I}$) and calculated accuracies in combination with all 100 fixed partitionings. For each of the 3 test configurations we determined the set of selected features maximising the average accuracies of $\mathcal{I}_{\text{test}}$ over all partitionings and report the results in Table 3. Note that in case of $\mathcal{F}_{\text{comp}}$ the feature selection was computationally demanding and we aborted the calculation after 48h for each of the 10 partitionings. At that time the first 40 best features were selected, explaining the slightly lower accuracies. Even if we directly compare the accuracies between the best 40 features of $\mathcal{F}_{\text{extc}}$ and $\mathcal{F}_{\text{comp}}$, the results are very similar. Furthermore, a comparison of the accuracies in Tab. 3 with the results in Tab. 2 shows only small differences and negligible changes in the overall performance.

Table 3. Best average accuracies obtained after feature selection in $\mathcal{F}_{\text{extc}}$ and $\mathcal{F}_{\text{comp}}$. The employed set of camera models during feature selection is indicated in brackets after each feature set and the depicted accuracies are calculated in combination with both sets of camera models.

model set	$\mathcal{I}$	SFFS on feature set		
		$\mathcal{F}_{\text{extc}}$ ($\mathcal{M}_{\text{red}}$)	$\mathcal{F}_{\text{extc}}$ ($\mathcal{M}_{\text{all}}$)	$\mathcal{F}_{\text{comp}}$ ($\mathcal{M}_{\text{red}}$)
$\mathcal{M}_{\text{red}}$ ($w_{\text{DB8,col}}$)	$\mathcal{I}_{\text{test}}$	97.72% (1.27)	**97.79%** (0.95)	97.05% (1.17)
$\mathcal{M}_{\text{all}}$ ($w_{\text{DB8,col}}$)	$\mathcal{I}_{\text{test}}$	92.89% (1.93)	**93.59%** (1.96)	91.49% (2.13)
$\mathcal{M}_{\text{red}}$ ($w_{\text{DB8,col}}$)	$\mathcal{I}_{\text{val}}$	96.08% (1.60)	95.97% (1.11)	**96.16%** (1.20)
$\mathcal{M}_{\text{all}}$ ($w_{\text{DB8,col}}$)	$\mathcal{I}_{\text{val}}$	90.77% (2.50)	**91.68%** (2.31)	90.47% (2.08)

Feature selection might help to increase the overall performance in case of a specific partitioning of $\mathcal{I}$, but it is difficult to find a universally valid reduced set of features. For the following tests only results employing $\mathcal{F}_{\text{extc}}$ are reported. Table 4 gives an example of the average detection rate for each camera model employing $\mathcal{I}_{\text{val}}$ ($\mathcal{I}_{\text{test}}$ is used in cases where only one camera model is available). The concrete detection rate depends on the camera model and, for example, images acquired with a Nikon S710 or a Ricoh GX 100 can be reliably identified with low false acceptance rate. For cameras like the Sony T77 the accuracy drops to 84.9% due to a higher similarity to camera models of the same manufacturer W170 and H50 as well as as a higher similarity to the Panasonic DMC-FZ50.

The next Section presents a detailed analysis of the similarity between different camera models and between devices of one camera model. Using $\mathcal{F}_{\text{extc}}$ we determined $\gamma = 2^{-9}$ and $C = 2^8$ as appropriate parameters for all 100 partitionings to decrease computational requirements.

4.3   Intra- and Inter-camera Model Similarity

The ability to separate between different camera models and not between different devices is a basic requirement for all camera model identification schemes. Therefore, characteristics should be chosen in a way that the intra-camera model similarity is high, i.e., feature values of devices of the same model are similar. In contrast, the inter-camera model similarity between different camera models should be minimised.

To give a visualisation of intra- and inter-camera model similarity between all employed 74 devices for $\mathcal{F}_{extc}$, we calculated for each device the centroid over all corresponding feature values. Applying multi-dimensional scaling the centroids mapped to 2D are depicted in Fig. 3. The visualisation clearly shows a spatial grouping of devices of the same camera model and supports the assumption, that the employed features are able to separate between camera models.

In a more detailed plot in Fig. 4, we illustrate the dissimilarity between feature values of single images of different camera models together with the similarity between devices of the same model. In Figure 4a the separation between the two camera models Nikon S710 and Sony T77 is clearly possible, while it is not possible to separate between different devices. In contrast, the dissimilarity of images made with camera models of the same manufacturer is sometimes lower and makes a separation more difficult. Figure 4b depicts an example for this case.

To investigate intra- and inter-camera model similarity in more detail, we trained the feature-based camera model identification scheme for each device of one camera model − contrary to its original purpose. We calculated average results iterating over the fixed set of 100 partitionings. Table 5 shows the results for separating between all devices of Nikon S710, Sony T77 and Sony W170. Similar to the observations in Fig. 4, a clear separation between Nikon and Sony camera models is possible. Furthermore, discriminating between the camera models T77 and W170 both manufactured by Sony are slightly worse and indicate possible manufacturer-specific dependencies. In all cases it is not possible to separate between devices of the same camera model with acceptable accuracy.

The two devices of the SLR camera model Nikon D200 are a noteworthy exception. In case of these two devices, device identification using feature-based camera model identification is indeed possible with high accuracy (see Tab. 6). In contrast, the four devices of the SLR model D70/D70s are indistinguishable from each other. Reconsidering the detailed results in Tab. 4, the low intra-camera model similarity between the D200 devices might explain the low detection rate of 80% in detecting the correct camera model.

4.4   Influence of the Number of Images, Devices and Models

The available resources during a forensic investigation are limited in terms of time and money. Consequently, it is important to know how many images and devices have to be considered to train a feature-based camera model scheme for a specific set of models reliably. Furthermore, it is important to consider relations between the number of questioned camera models and the accuracy in detecting the correct camera model.

Table 4. Average detection rates for $\mathcal{L}_{val}$ and, if only one device is available, for $\mathcal{L}_{test}$ employing $\mathcal{F}_{extc}$ and all 100 fixed partitionings of $\mathcal{L}$. Models with only one device available are indicated by (*). The average accuracy is 90.93% for $\mathcal{L}_{val}$, 93.12% for $\mathcal{L}_{test}$ and 91.18% for the depicted combination of $\mathcal{L}_{val}$ and $\mathcal{L}_{test}$.

model	504	733	830	505	530	I55	I70	A64	Z15	J50	M10	S71	D20	D70	μ	FZ5	A40	W60	DCZ	GX	732	L74	NV	H50	T77	W17
															identified as											
DC-504*	**88.0**	-	-	-	6.8	0.6	-	-	-	-	-	0.2	1.2	1.2	-	-	0.1	-	1.8	-	-	-	-	-	-	-
DC-733s*	-	**92.6**	0.2	-	0.1	-	1.5	-	1.4	-	0.3	-	-	0.6	-	-	-	0.2	0.1	0.6	-	2.2	0.1	-	-	-
DC-830i*	-	0.5	**97.4**	-	0.2	-	0.1	-	0.8	0.6	-	-	0.2	-	0.1	0.1	-	-	-	-	-	0.1	-	-	-	-
505-X*	3.8	0.7	-	**87.6**	0.7	1.5	-	-	-	-	2.2	-	-	1.2	-	-	0.1	-	-	-	-	0.1	-	-	-	-
530s*	-	-	0.1	0.1	**90.2**	3.1	-	-	-	-	-	-	1.1	0.5	-	-	0.5	-	0.5	-	-	-	-	-	-	-
Ixus 55*	0.1	0.1	0.3	0.3	1.3	**94.9**	-	0.2	0.2	0.1	0.1	-	-	0.9	-	-	-	-	2.4	-	-	-	-	-	-	-
Ixus 70	-	6.0	0.6	0.1	0.1	0.1	**87.3**	-	-	-	-	-	-	1.9	3.3	-	-	-	-	-	-	3.5	-	-	-	-
A640*	-	2.5	2.4	-	1.5	-	-	**92.3**	-	-	0.2	-	0.9	-	-	-	0.3	-	-	-	-	-	0.9	-	0.1	-
Z150	-	-	-	-	0.1	-	-	-	**93.5**	-	0.3	0.1	0.4	0.2	-	0.2	-	-	0.1	-	-	-	0.2	-	0.1	-
J50	-	-	8.8	-	-	-	-	-	-	**90.3**	-	-	-	-	-	0.1	-	-	-	-	0.3	-	-	0.3	0.1	-
M1063	0.1	-	-	-	0.1	-	-	0.1	-	-	**98.9**	-	0.4	0.1	-	-	-	-	-	-	-	-	0.2	-	0.1	-
S710	-	-	-	-	-	-	-	0.2	-	-	0.1	**98.8**	-	-	-	0.4	0.3	-	-	-	-	-	0.2	-	-	-
D200	6.1	-	0.5	-	1.2	-	-	0.8	0.6	-	0.8	-	**80.2**	-	0.9	5.6	0.5	0.6	0.9	0.1	-	1.6	1.0	0.2	0.2	0.6
D70(s)	0.7	0.7	0.7	0.3	0.3	0.1	1.2	0.2	0.2	-	0.9	0.1	0.1	**92.5**	-	1.2	0.1	-	-	0.6	-	-	0.2	-	-	-
μ1050	-	0.7	0.8	-	0.1	-	-	3.4	0.1	0.3	0.1	-	0.2	-	**85.5**	-	4.5	-	0.1	0.6	-	-	2.6	-	-	-
F250	0.2	-	0.4	-	-	-	-	0.1	0.2	-	1.4	1.8	0.6	-	0.4	**90.2**	0.2	-	-	-	-	-	0.1	3.1	1.4	2.1
A40	1.5	-	-	-	1.1	-	-	0.5	0.2	-	1.1	-	0.2	-	-	0.2	**89.6**	0.1	-	1.8	-	-	1.2	-	0.1	0.1
W60*	0.1	-	-	-	-	-	-	0.2	0.2	0.6	0.1	-	0.4	-	6.7	0.4	-	**91.0**	-	-	-	-	0.2	-	-	-
DC25.9	-	-	0.1	4.6	0.1	2.3	-	0.2	-	-	-	-	-	1.2	-	-	-	-	**91.4**	-	-	-	-	-	-	-
GX100	0.1	0.2	0.1	0.1	0.5	-	-	-	-	1.1	0.2	-	0.1	-	0.8	-	0.2	-	0.2	**97.2**	-	-	0.1	0.2	0.1	0.9
732SXS	-	-	0.1	0.1	-	-	-	-	-	-	-	-	-	-	-	-	-	-	-	-	**97.2**	0.2	0.2	0.1	-	-
L74	4.3	-	0.6	0.6	-	-	1.7	-	-	-	0.2	-	-	1.6	-	-	-	-	-	-	-	**91.0**	-	-	-	-
NV15	0.1	-	-	-	0.5	-	0.4	2.6	0.1	0.2	0.3	-	1.4	-	4.1	2.5	0.1	0.2	-	1.2	-	-	**85.9**	-	0.2	-
H50	-	-	0.7	0.1	-	0.1	0.1	-	-	-	-	-	0.2	-	0.1	3.0	-	-	-	-	-	-	-	**92.7**	1.4	1.7
T77	-	-	0.1	-	-	-	-	0.1	0.3	0.2	-	-	0.6	-	0.1	6.5	-	-	0.5	-	-	-	0.2	2.9	**84.9**	3.6
W170	0.1	-	-	-	-	-	-	0.1	-	-	0.1	-	0.1	-	0.1	2.8	-	-	0.1	0.1	-	-	3.5	3.5	3.6	**89.5**

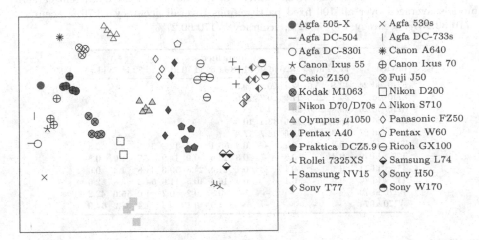

Fig. 3. Visualisation of intra- and inter-camera model similarity. The centroid of all feature values of all images of each device is mapped to 2D using multi-dimensional scaling and different devices of one camera model are depicted by the same symbol. Devices of the same camera model are closer to each other whereas devices of different models are farther apart.

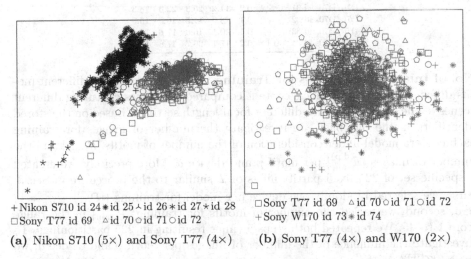

+Nikon S710 id 24 ✳ id 25 ⅄ id 26 ✳ id 27 ✶ id 28   □ Sony T77 id 69   △ id 70 ○ id 71 ○ id 72
□ Sony T77 id 69   △ id 70 ○ id 71 ○ id 72   +Sony W170 id 73 ✳ id 74

(a) Nikon S710 (5×) and Sony T77 (4×)   **(b)** Sony T77 (4×) and W170 (2×)

Fig. 4. Visualisation of the similarity of feature values between all images of pairs of camera models using the two most distinctive principal components. Different symbols of the same colour indicate different devices of one camera model. Camera models are visually separable, but a differentiation between devices of the same model is not possible.

Table 5. Intra- and inter-camera similarity between devices of three different camera models averaged over all 100 fixed partitionings (overall accuracy 43.76%, accuracy S710 32.23%, accuracy T77 49.92%, accuracy W170 60.27%).

device		identified as									
		id 24	id 25	id 26	id 27	id 28	id 69	id 70	id 71	id 72	id 73	id 74
S710	id 24	**42.8**	15.0	12.1	20.2	9.8	-	-	-	-	-	-
S710	id 25	24.1	21.5	17.9	20.7	15.9	-	-	-	-	-	-
S710	id 26	19.8	20.6	**26.4**	14.6	18.5	-	-	-	-	-	-
S710	id 27	26.7	17.3	12.6	**33.1**	10.3	-	-	-	-	-	-
S710	id 28	15.3	16.0	16.6	14.7	**37.4**	-	-	-	-	-	-
T77	id 69	0.3	0.2	0.1	-	0.4	**55.1**	17.6	12.8	10.3	2.2	0.8
T77	id 70	0.4	-	0.3	-	0.3	23.6	**50.9**	14.9	7.7	1.0	0.8
T77	id 71	0.1	-	0.1	-	0.1	21.4	24.8	**39.3**	11.8	1.8	0.6
T77	id 72	0.2	-	0.1	-	0.4	16.4	10.5	11.6	**54.4**	3.8	2.6
W170	id 73	-	-	-	-	-	0.8	0.2	0.2	1.0	**55.6**	42.2
W170	id 74	-	-	-	-	-	1.0	0.1	0.3	1.4	32.2	**64.9**

Table 6. Intra- and inter-camera similarity between devices of camera models D70/D70s and D200 averaged over all 100 fixed partitionings (overall accuracy 60.35%, accuracy D200 95.82%, accuracy D70/D70s 42.61%).

device		identified as					
		id 29	id 30	id 31	id 32	id 33	id 34
D200	id 29	**95.4**	4.5	-	-	-	-
D200	id 30	3.8	**96.2**	-	-	-	-
D70/D70s	id 31	-	0.2	**34.2**	25.3	22.0	18.3
D70/D70s	id 32	-	0.1	23.0	**44.5**	16.8	15.6
D70/D70s	id 33	-	0.1	20.1	16.6	**47.6**	15.6
D70/D70s	id 34	0.1	0.2	17.1	20.7	17.8	**44.1**

No. of Images and Devices for Training. Pictures taken from different motifs differ significantly in image content compared to images capturing different scenes of the same motif with different focal length settings. Based on the stored identifiers in the database, we investigate the number of images for training each camera model under consideration of the number of motifs $|\mathcal{P}_{train}|$ and the number of images $|\mathcal{I}_{train}^{(d,p)}|$ per motif p and device d. More precisely, we created a specific set of 225 fixed partitionings of $\mathcal{I}$ similar to the procedure in Sec. 3: First, we selected randomly one device per model for training ($|\mathcal{D}_{train,test}^{(m)}| = 1$) and, second, we varied the number of motifs for training $|\mathcal{P}_{train}|$ in the range from 1 to 45. We repeated both steps 5 times resulting in 225 partitionings. To investigate the influence of the number of images per motif p and device d, we varied $|\mathcal{I}_{train}^{(d,p)}|$ in the range from 1 to the maximum number available. Note that there are 47 motifs for camera models in set A available, whereas set B only holds 30 or 36 motifs, depending on the camera model. To keep distinct motifs for training and testing, we left always a minimum of 3 testing motifs for each camera model ($|\mathcal{P}_{test,val}| \geq 3$).

Figure 5 illustrates the relation between the accuracy and the number of images for training for $\mathcal{M}_{all}$ and $\mathcal{M}_{red}$. The depicted accuracy is averaged over all

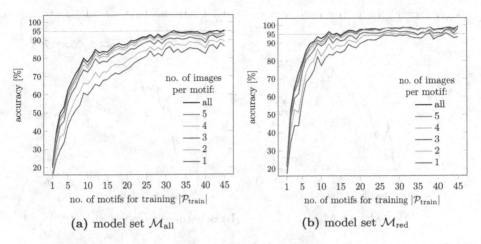

(a) model set $\mathcal{M}_{\text{all}}$ **(b)** model set $\mathcal{M}_{\text{red}}$

Fig. 5. Relation between the number of motifs available for training $|\mathcal{P}_{\text{train}}|$ and the accuracy for $\mathcal{I}_{\text{val}}$. Additionally, the influence of the number of images per motif p (and per device d) $|\mathcal{I}_{\text{train}}^{(d,p)}|$ is depicted.

5 fixed sets of training devices $\mathcal{D}_{\text{train,test}}$. Employing the smaller set of camera models $\mathcal{M}_{\text{red}}$ results in a faster increase of accuracy compared to $\mathcal{M}_{\text{all}}$. The influence of the number of different motifs is higher than the influence of the number of images per motif. Nevertheless, adding images with different camera settings is still important to achieve the maximum possible accuracy. After adding 30 motifs in case of $\mathcal{M}_{\text{all}}$ and 20 motifs in case of $\mathcal{M}_{\text{red}}$, we observe only a minor increase in accuracy. Nonetheless, it is important to employ a notable number of images capturing different motifs to get best detection rates. Depending on the number of camera models considered during an investigation, we suggest $|\mathcal{I}_{\text{train}}^{(d,p)}| \geq 3$ acquired with different camera settings for a minimum of $|\mathcal{P}_{\text{train}}| \geq 30$ motifs to get reasonable accuracies. Whenever possible, the number of motifs should be increased.

In another experiment, we investigated the relation between the number of devices $|\mathcal{D}_{\text{train,test}}^{(m)}|$ and motifs $|\mathcal{P}_{\text{train}}|$ for training. We used the previously introduced set of 225 fixed partitionings and selected randomly 1 up to 4 devices for training, where available. In case of camera models with more than one device in the database, we always left a minimum of one distinct device for validation ($|\mathcal{D}_{\text{val}}^{(m)}| \geq 1$).

The average results are depicted in Fig. 6 for $\mathcal{M}_{\text{all}}$ and a set of 15 camera models including 3 or more devices per model. Different to the previous results on the influence of the number of motifs and images per motif, increasing the number of devices has a negligible influence on the accuracy. Consequently, practical investigation should focus available resources on the acquisition of enough images per camera model covering different motifs and camera settings. Borrowing or purchasing more than one device per camera model is less important regarding the average case. Reconsidering the results on intra- and inter-camera

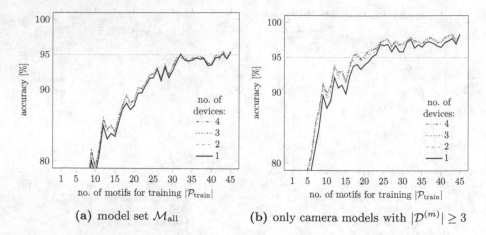

(a) model set $\mathcal{M}_{\text{all}}$ \qquad\qquad (b) only camera models with $|\mathcal{D}^{(m)}| \geq 3$

Fig. 6. Relation between number of motifs $|\mathcal{P}_{\text{train}}|$, devices per model $|\mathcal{D}^{(m)}_{\text{train,test}}|$ and accuracy for $\mathcal{I}_{\text{val}}$. Increasing the number of devices per camera model has a negligible influence on the accuracy.

model similarity of the Nikon D200 in Sec. 4.3, it might be still necessary to employ more than one device in some cases.

No. of Camera Models. Comparing the results depicted in Fig. 5a and b clearly indicates a decrease in accuracy when a larger set of camera models is considered. To investigate the influence of the number of camera models in more detail, we conducted two experiments employing the 100 fixed partitionings introduced in Sec. 3. Starting with $\mathcal{M}_{\text{all}}$, in the first experiment we removed models one by one in order to maximise the accuracy on the reduced set. In the second experiment we did the opposite and removed models in order to minimise the accuracy. With both experiments we try to gauge the range of correct identification results in relation to the number of employed camera models in a good and bad scenario.

Figure 7 depicts the average accuracy for $\mathcal{I}_{\text{test}}$ and $\mathcal{I}_{\text{val}}$ in relation to the number of removed camera models for the two experiments over 100 fixed partitionings. Furthermore, we determined the number of occurrences each camera model was removed first, second and so on, and specified the camera models with the highest count on the x-axis of the two plots. Reducing the number of camera models considered during an investigation does not necessarily increase the accuracy in detecting the correct camera model. In fact, an inconvenient combination of camera models can even for small sets result in low detection rates. It might be contradictory at first glance, that removing a camera model results in a lower accuracy, but by doing this only worse separable camera models remain and the average accuracy decreases.

We plotted also the accuracy of correctly identifying the set of snapshot images mentioned in Sec. 3. These images are photographed freehand employing many different focal length settings, and were acquired in several cases in dark

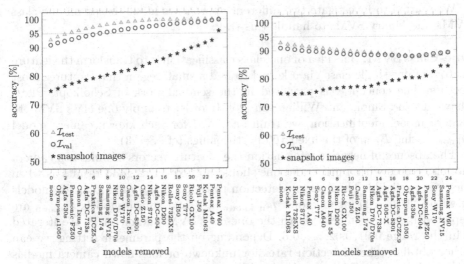

(a) models removed to maximise accuracy **(b)** models removed to minimise accuracy

Fig. 7. Relation between number of camera models considered during an investigation and accuracy. Depending on the combination of camera models in question, the accuracy can be also low for small sets of models.

environments with active flash. The depicted accuracy is considerably less compared to $\mathcal{I}_{test}$ and $\mathcal{I}_{val}$. To study the cause of this bad result, we trained the feature-based camera model identification scheme for all 8 camera models where snapshot images are available. We either employed the standard motifs or the snapshot images of one device of each camera model for training. Similar to Fig. 7 the average accuracy for correctly identifying the employed model to acquire a snapshot image is quite low (78.4%) when we employ our standard motifs for training. However, if we flip training and validation data and use all snapshot images of one device of each camera model for training, we get a high accuracy (93.1%) for correctly assigning standard motifs to the corresponding camera model. The results emphasise the importance of using different camera settings during the preparation of images for training feature-based camera model identification.

5 Camera-Model Identification in Open Sets

Although forensic investigators may put considerable effort into the creation of a large reference database for training, it is very unlikely that this database will ever be comprehensive. Therefore a residual risk remains that the camera model of a given image is not in the database. For critical forensic applications (i.e., in criminal court), this case should be detected with almost certainty to avoid potential false accusations under all circumstances.

We started to investigate two different approaches in [20] based on one-class SVMs and binary SVMs to handle this task:

One-Class SVM. The idea of one-class classification is to transform the feature vectors of one single class via a kernel to find a small region that captures most vectors. The concept was proposed in the seminal work of Schölkopf, Platt, Shawe-Taylor, Smola and Williamson [26]. In order to apply one-class SVMs to camera model identification, we train one SVM for each known camera model m_{known} using $\mathcal{I}_{train}$ of the fixed 100 partitionings (cf., Sec. 3).

The absence of negative information (i.e., feature vectors of unknown camera models) comes with a price, and one should not expect as good results as when they are available. The average detection rates using $\mathcal{I}_{val}$ (and $\mathcal{I}_{test}$ for models m with $|\mathcal{D}^{(m)}| = 1$) for unknown $m_{unknown\ (real)}$ and known models m_{known} are depicted in Fig. 8a in relation to the one-class SVM parameter ν. We iterated ν in the range $0.01, 0.02, \ldots, 0.6$. Depending on the parameter setting we can either obtain higher detection rates for unknown or for known camera models and reach a trade-off between both with $\nu = 0.17$ and 76% average accuracy.

An alternative approach is to optimise ν for each camera model separately. Figure 8b visualises the performance for selected models using ROC curves. Here, true and false positive rates indicate the percentage of images assigned to a known model correctly or incorrectly. The results for models Casio EX-Z150 and Agfa DC-830i show the best and worst case for our employed set of camera models ($\mathcal{M}_{all}$) and ROC curves of all other camera models are in between. Ideally, we want very low false positive rates (high probability to identify $m_{unknown\ (real)}$) and high true positive rates (high probability to identify m_{known}). However, the figure indicates that not all observed results are convincing with respect to practical scenarios in this regard.

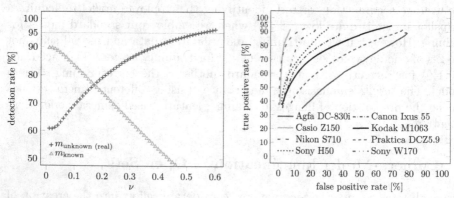

(a) detection rates in relation to ν averaged over all models $\mathcal{M}_{all}$

(b) ROC curves for selected models (curves are incomplete due to the chosen range of ν)

Fig. 8. Averaged results using one-class SVMs and 100 fixed partitionings of $\mathcal{I}$

Binary SVM. In addition to one-class SVMs, also binary SVMs can be exploited in the open-set problem. In Section 4 the multi-class problem is solved by creating single binary SVMs for all pairs of different classes (one-versus-one) and a voting scheme determines the most probable class (cf. Sec. 3). The general lack of training data for unknown camera models makes the application of the standard multi-class classification scheme difficult. One solution to find an approximation of unknown models could be to use known models as samples of unknown models.

To experimentally investigate this approach, we iterate over all combinations of each one known and one unknown camera model, m_{known} and $m_{unknown\ (real)}$, respectively. Depending on the combination, we sample training data for unknown models from all remaining models $m_{unknown\ (train)} \in \mathcal{M}_{all}/\{m_{known},\ m_{unknown\ (real)}\}$ and employ the fixed set of 100 partitionings of $\mathcal{I}$. Figure 9 summarises average detection rates for correctly identifying our two trained classes m_{known}, $m_{unknown\ (train)}$ and the 'real' unknown models $m_{unknown\ (real)}$ in relation to the selected known camera model m_{known}. Depending on the known camera model, detecting trained models m_{known}, $m_{unknown\ (train)}$ works well. Compared to the results in Sec. 4, the detection rates for known camera models are lower because of the differences in the implementation. On average also a reliable detection of $m_{unknown\ (real)}$ is possible, but in practice especially worst cases need attention. Depending on the combination of m_{known} and $m_{unknown\ (real)}$ the correct identification of unknown models is sometimes much more difficult and the detection results are not always convincing. For example, detecting $m_{unknown\ (real)}$ = Nikon S710 results in the lowest detection rate (7.33%) in our test scenario when we trained a binary SVM with m_{known} = Pentax A40. In the opposite combination the detection rate for the unknown

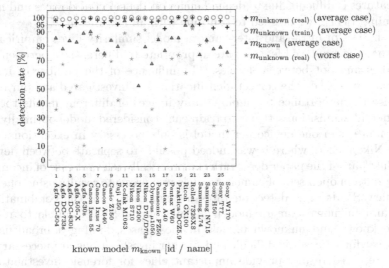

Fig. 9. Averaged results using binary SVMs and 100 fixed partitionings of $\mathcal{I}$

model is considerably better (70.74%, $m_{unknown\ (real)}$ = Pentax A40, m_{known} = Nikon S710). Note, detection rates for known models remain stable even in the worst case scenario and do not decrease by more than 3 percentage points.

Overall, the experiments considering open sets reveal the difficulties to handle unknown camera models in practice. While average detection rates of binary SVMs for known and unknown camera models are promising, detailed investigations illustrate that the approximation of unknown models with samples of known models is prone to be incomplete. Hence, worst case detection rates might be considerably lower. Similarly, the absence of training data for unknown models in case of one-class SVMs results in unsatisfactory identification results. In summary, we see both approaches as very first attempts to handle unknown camera models. Further research is necessary to improve the prevention of false accusations.

6 Concluding Remarks

This paper complements existing work on feature-based forensic camera model identification by an experimental in-depth analysis on a large set of 26 camera models and altogether 74 devices. We investigated different sets of features known from the literature and achieved the best results using the 82 features of the extended colour feature set $\mathcal{F}_{extc}$. While the improvement by adding binary similarity measures BSM was negligible in our test scenario, the computational requirements increased considerably for the set of all 26 camera models. In practice, the optimal feature set depends on the employed set of models and maybe also on the type of cameras (digital still camera or mobile phone camera). Furthermore, our investigations on feature selection show, that finding a set of optimal features is difficult due to dependencies on the selected devices and motifs for training. Hence, we decided to continue with all features in $\mathcal{F}_{extc}$.

Our analysis of intra- and inter-camera model similarity gives empirical evidence, that the employed features are appropriate to differentiate between camera models and not between devices. The influence of the number of images, devices and models on the correct identification was investigated and our results emphasise the importance to employ many images of different motifs together with different acquisition settings to train each considered model optimally. Employing more than one device per model is only necessary in exceptional cases like the Nikon D200, where it was indeed possible to separate between devices.

The last part of the paper deals with the practically relevant case of incomplete training data in open sets of camera models and presents results using one-class and binary SVMs. The detection rates depend clearly on the combination of known and unknown camera models. While binary SVMs enable to reliably separate known and unknown models in most cases, finding a broad enough training set for all cases is difficult and further investigations are necessary.

The presented results provide important clues for forensic investigators to select appropriate parameters for training a specific set of camera models as well as to assess detection results in a real case. A direction for future work is a detailed analysis of the influence of image processing on the identification results. First investigations presented at DAGM 2010 [20] are worse compared to the results known from previous literature [16,17] and need further attention to identify robust subsets of features. Also different JPEG compression settings implemented in digital cameras may obscure a correct model identification and call for a careful investigation under controlled settings.

Calculating and analysing the features for all employed images required more than 15,000 hours of computation time. Therefore, supplementary material is made available via 'Dresden Image Database' website (https://forensics.inf. tu-dresden.de/ddimgdb/publications/modelid). We hope this not only saves ressources in the development of new forensic techniques but als provides a good starting point for introducing students to image forensics research.

Acknowledgements. The author thanks Nicolas Cebron and Rainer Böhme for fruitful discussions on machine learning and the detection of unknown camera models during the preparation of the extended abstract for DAGM 2010 [20]. We thank also Matthias Kirchner for commenting the final manuscript.

This project was partly funded by the German Research Foundation (Deutsche Forschungsgemeinschaft, DFG). Computational resources to calculate the experimental results were provided by the centre for high-performance computing (ZIH) at our university.

References

1. Böhme, R., Freiling, F., Gloe, T., Kirchner, M.: Multimedia Forensics Is Not Computer Forensics. In: Geradts, Z.J.M.H., Franke, K.Y., Veenman, C.J. (eds.) IWCF 2009. LNCS, vol. 5718, pp. 90–103. Springer, Heidelberg (2009)
2. Khanna, N., Mikkilineni, A.K., Chiu, G.T.C., Allebach, J.P., Delp, E.J.: Forensic classification of imaging sensor types. In: Delp, E.J., Wong, P.W. (eds.) Proceedings of SPIE: Security and Watermarking of Multimedia Content IX, vol. 6505, p. 65050U (2007)
3. Lyu, S., Farid, H.: How realistic is photorealistic? IEEE Transactions on Signal Processing 53(2), 845–850 (2005)
4. Fridrich, J.: Digital image forensics. IEEE Signal Processing Magazine 26(2), 26–37 (2009)
5. Gloe, T., Franz, E., Winkler, A.: Forensics for flatbed scanners. In: Delp, E.J., Wong, P.W. (eds.) Proceedings of SPIE: Security, Steganography, and Watermarking of Multimedia Contents IX, vol. 6505, p. 65051I (2007)
6. Gou, H., Swaminathan, A., Wu, M.: Robust scanner identification based on noise features. In: Delp, E.J., Wong, P.W. (eds.) Proceedings of SPIE: Security and Watermarking of Multimedia Content IX, vol. 6505, p. 65050S (2007)
7. Khanna, N., Mikkikineni, A.K., Chiu, G.T.C., Allebach, J.P., Delp, E.J.: Scanner identification using sensor pattern noise. In: Delp, E.J., Wong, P.W. (eds.) Proceedings of SPIE: Security and Watermarking of Multimedia Content IX, vol. 6505, p. 65051K (2007)
8. Goljan, M., Fridrich, J., Filler, T.: Large scale test of sensor fingerprint camera identification. In: Delp, E.J., Dittmann, J., Memon, N., Wong, P.W. (eds.) Proceedings of SPIE: Media Forensics and Security XI, vol. 7254, pp. 7254–18 (2009)

9. Johnson, M.K., Farid, H.: Exposing digital forgeries through chromatic aberration. In: Proceedings of the Multimedia and Security Workshop (MM&Sec 2006), pp. 48–55 (2006)

10. Gloe, T., Borowka, K., Winkler, A.: Efficient estimation and large-scale evaluation of lateral chromatic aberration for digital image forensics. In: Memon, N.D., Dittmann, J., Alattar, A.M., Delp, E.J. (eds.) Proceedings of SPIE: Media Forensics and Security II, vol. 7541, pp. 7541–7 (2010)

11. Swaminathan, A., Wu, M., Liu, K.J.R.: Nonintrusive component forensics of visual sensors using output images. IEEE Transactions on Information Forensics and Security 2(1), 91–106 (2007)

12. Cao, H., Kot, A.C.: Accurate detection of demosaicing regularity for digital image forensics. IEEE Transactions on Information Forensics and Security 4(4), 899–910 (2009)

13. Farid, H.: Digital image ballistics from JPEG quantization: A followup study. Technical Report TR2008-638, Department of Computer Science, Dartmouth College, Hanover, NH, USA (2008)

14. Kee, E., Johnson, M.K., Farid, H.: Digital image authentication from JPEG headers. IEEE Transactions on Information Forensics and Security 6(3), 1066–1075 (2011)

15. Kharrazi, M., Sencar, H.T., Memon, N.: Blind source camera identification. In: Proceedings of the 2004 IEEE International Conference on Image Processing (ICIP 2004), pp. 709–712 (2004)

16. Çeliktutan, O., Avcibas, İ., Sankur, B.: Blind identification of cellular phone cameras. In: Delp, E.J., Wong, P.W. (eds.) Proceedings of SPIE: Security and Watermarking of Multimedia Content IX, vol. 6505, p. 65051H (2007)

17. Çeliktutan, O., Sankur, B., Avcibas, İ.: Blind identification of source cell-phone model. IEEE Transactions on Information Forensics and Security 3(3), 553–566 (2008)

18. Gloe, T., Borowka, K., Winkler, A.: Feature-Based Camera Model Identification Works in Practice – Results of a Comprehensive Evaluation Study. In: Katzenbeisser, S., Sadeghi, A.-R. (eds.) IH 2009. LNCS, vol. 5806, pp. 262–276. Springer, Heidelberg (2009)

19. Gloe, T., Böhme, R.: The 'Dresden Image Database' for benchmarking digital image forensics. In: Proceedings of the 25th Symposium on Applied Computing (ACM SAC), vol. 2, pp. 1585–1591 (2010)

20. Gloe, T., Cebron, N., Böhme, R.: An ML perspective on feature-based forensic camera model identification. In: DAGM Workshop Pattern Recognition for IT Security, Darmstadt, Germany, September 21 (2010)

21. Farid, H., Lyu, S.: Higher-order wavelet statistics and their application to digital forensics. In: IEEE Workshop on Statistical Analysis in Computer Vision (2003)

22. Avcıbaş, İ., Sankur, B., Sayood, K.: Statistical evaluation of image quality measures. Journal of Electronic Imaging 11(2), 206–223 (2002)

23. Avcibas, İ., Kharrazi, M., Memon, N.D., Sankur, B.: Image steganalysis with binary similarity measures. EURASIP Journal on Applied Signal Processing 2005(17), 2749–2757 (2005)

24. Chang, C.C., Lin, C.J.: LIBSVM: A library for support vector machines. Software (2001), http://www.csie.ntu.edu.tw/~cjlin/libsvm

25. Pudil, P., Novovičová, J., Kittler, J.: Floating search methods in feature selection. Pattern Recognition Letters 15(11), 1119–1125 (1994)

26. Schölkopf, B., Platt, J.C., Shawe-Taylor, J., Smola, A.J., Williamson, R.C.: Estimating the support of a high-dimensional distribution. Neural Computation 13(7), 1443–1471 (2001)

Watermark Embedding Using Audio Fingerprinting

Sascha Zmudzinski, Martin Steinebach, and Moazzam Butt

Fraunhofer Institute for Secure Information Technology SIT,
Rheinstr 75, 64295 Darmstadt, Germany
{zmudzinski,butt,steinebach}@sit.fraunhofer.de

Abstract. Digital watermarking is a common technique in multimedia security for copyright protection and data authentication. Embedding a digital watermark into a media file is often computationally demanding as multiple operations take place within the process to ensure a high level of perceived quality of the marked copy and a high robustness of the embedded watermark. State of the art watermarking algorithms require time consuming spectral transformation operations as well as windowing and perceptual models for masking the embedded watermark. Our new concept is to set up a collection of pre-computed watermarking signals and mix them with the cover signal for fast and simple embedding. To ensure that the watermark signal is well suited for the embedding position with respect to masking, we suggest using audio fingerprinting technology as matching mechanism. Test results show that our approach in able to watermark content using such proposed lookup collection.

Keywords: Digital watermarking, audio fingerprinting, perceptual hashing.

1 Motivation

Digital watermarking has become a common procedure in commercial media applications, be it audio, video, single image or e-book. Some of these applications require the watermarking algorithm to work in real-time with minimal delay; many demand even faster embedding (e.g. in video-on-demand or mp3 download shops).

This challenge can be addressed with different mechanisms depending on the use case. While least significant bit embedding algorithms are fast and simple to implement and require almost no computational power, their usability for most watermarking applications is minimal. Here the only way to speed up the embedding process is either to provide more computational power or to design more efficient watermarking strategies. The latter approach is not trivial, as watermarking often relies on computational demanding transformations and complex perceptual models.

In this work, we describe a novel alternative path to watermark embedding, providing a hybrid approach between container pre-processing and efficient watermarking. The basic idea is to create a container with pre-calculated watermarked signals from content which can be expected to be similar to that found in the media stream to be watermarked and use this container as a *lookup collection*.

Y.Q. Shi (Ed.): Transactions on DHMS VIII, LNCS 7228, pp. 63–79, 2012.

2   Background and State of the Art

In this section we introduce the two main mechanisms utilized and combined in our work, namely digital watermarking and fingerprinting. For both, we provide a general overview as well as a more detailed discussion of challenges and known solutions relevant for our work.

2.1   Digital Watermarking

Digital watermarking is a technique for embedding information in multimedia data [CMB2002]. It is based on information hiding techniques similar to steganographic approaches with the overall goal to embed information into a cover signal, usually multimedia data. The term digital watermarking was used for the first time by *Tirkel et al* in [OST1994], actually written in two words: "*water mark*".

2.1.1   Basic Watermarking Principles

A digital watermark is a perceptually transparent pattern inserted in digital data using an embedding algorithm and an embedding key. A detection algorithm using the appropriate detection key can retrieve the watermark information. In most approaches the embedding and detection keys are secret.

Typical watermarking applications are copyright protection, data authentication, broadcast monitoring, or enabling innovative multimedia services. Dependent on the application, the embedded watermark represents information about

- the protected media itself (e.g. "This mp3 contains song X"), or
- its copyright owner (e.g. "Copyright owned by music label Y"), or
- the recipient of an individual copy (e.g. "This mp3 file purchased and downloaded by user Z"), or
- arbitrary data annotation (e.g. meta data, time codes, advertisement info or authentication codes).

Digital watermarking algorithms use a number of assisting technologies for embedding information into media files, for example:

- Perceptual models are used for ensuring the resulting quality of the marked cover by identifying areas in the cover where information can be hidden without degrading the perceived quality of the cover. Usage of a perceptual model enables transparent embedding for most covers, but may lead to a disability of embedding watermarks in certain material with problematic characteristics.
- Signal transformations like Fourier transformation or Wavelet transformation are applied if the cover signal is not provided in a domain suitable for watermark embedding. Then, a transformation is needed to calculate the spectrum of the cover. This spectrum is then modified by the watermarking algorithm and re-transformed to the original domain. Signal transformations often have the highest computational cost within the different steps of a watermarking algorithm.

Both perceptual model and signal transformation lead to a high computational complexity of the watermarking algorithm. This can become problematic if on-the-fly embedding, for example during online sales or video conferencing, is required. Therefore a number of strategies for speeding up the embedding process have been introduced.

2.1.2   Speeding up Watermarking Embedding

In transaction watermarking at online stores, *container* strategies can be applied to speed up the embedding process [SZF2006]. Here, for every media, a slow one-time pre-processing step takes place, creating a so-called watermarking container. From the container individual copies can be rendered by assembling the pre-processed data in the container in a copy-and-paste-manner very quickly, e.g. 3,000 times faster than playback speed in the case of mp3.

But if watermarking is applied at *live* content streams, watermarking based on pre-processing may be the inappropriate strategy, especially if there is only need for one watermarking message to be embedded into the stream. This could be the case in telephone or video communication, in surveillance camera streams or in copyright watermarking for broadcast signals. In that case, one approach for improving the speed of watermark embedding are so-called "bit stream embedders" [KCLI +2007] where transformation operations are saved by working on already transformed compressed media data.

Other known strategies are not based on speeding up the core embedder, but using an environment, for example a Grid or Cloud architecture, for distributing the computational cost on multiple computers or a Client-Server strategy where the embedding process is divided an a computational complex public stage at the Client and a computational simple stage at the Server [SHW2007].

2.2   Fingerprinting

Fingerprinting is a content-based retrieval method, often based on modeling human perception. For example, audio fingerprinting algorithms map an audio data segment of arbitrary length to a short message digest or content identifier. Similar approaches are known under the name *robust hashing* or *perceptional hashing* for audio (and video or image data, resp.). The term audio fingerprinting here shall not be confused with so-called *fingerprint watermarking* or *collusion-secure fingerprint coding* approaches that are resistant to security attacks on watermarking by a collusion of several attackers.

Unlike cryptographic hashes, fingerprints show certain robustness to moderate transformations of the audio data. That is, two audio segments that are acoustically similar to a Human, should have identical or similar fingerprints, even if the audio segments are not binary identical.

Content-based matching of audio data by fingerprinting can also be seen a *pattern recognition* challenge:

- The audio data is first acquired using a recording device, e.g. microphone, analog-to-digital conversion.

- Then, pre-processing is applied to the data, e.g. windowing, spectral transformation (DCT, DFT), data reduction.
- An appropriate feature extraction is done by extracting acoustically relevant features and pruning irrelevant features. Examples are statistical properties from the audio in the time or spectral domain.
- The extracted features are subject to further post-processing, e.g. to obtain a binary fingerprint identifier from continuous feature values.
- At a later point, one fingerprint is matched against a set of fingerprints derived from a set of audio files to test if the source of the fingerprint is an element of this set. This matching process is fuzzy and requires an estimation of similarity.

Usually, these algorithms in use in commercial systems for broadcast monitoring, music recommendation and to prevent that copyright protected audio material is uploaded to websites or peer-to-peer networks. One application is identifying the title of an unknown music song that is recorded from a loudspeaker using a microphone or cell phone, e.g. provided by the *Shazam[1]* or *Gracenote/Sony[2]* service. For example, the fingerprint algorithm presented by *Haitsma et al.* [HaKa2001, HaOK2001] features a 256 bit fingerprint from every three second audio segment. That fingerprint can be used for matching a given audio segment against a fingerprint database from music songs for music recommendation.

2.3 Fingerprinting-Based Support for Digital Watermarking

Besides the application fields mentioned in the previous chapter, audio fingerprinting has a number of applications also in the context of digital watermarking for different purposes [FG2000]:

- Indexing for informed/non-blind watermarking: When a watermarking algorithm requires the original medium to be available to detect the watermark from a marked copy, the audio fingerprint can help to identify the required original
- Payload for integrity protection: Here the audio fingerprint is stored as the watermark information to provide a content-based description of the original content.
- Key generator: The audio fingerprint of the original is used as the secret watermark key during embedding. If the original is changed, the audio fingerprint also changes and the watermark cannot be detected due to the wrong key given by the audio fingerprint. This can be used for integrity verification.
- Synchronization: The audio fingerprint is used as an index to identify positions within the marked content where the watermark has been

---

[1] www.shazam.com (URL verified January 2012).
[2] www.gracenote.com (URL verified January 2012).

embedded [HKM2005]. The audio fingerprints are often stored within a separate database. Approaches without the need of an external database are also known [SZN2006].

Beyond the applications listed before, we will show how fingerprinting can act as another supporting mechanism for watermarking.

3   Concept for Watermark Embedding Controlled by Fingerprinting

One can assume that watermark embedding and masking are controlled by perceptual models which provide a high degree of abstraction from the actual audio content. Thus, acoustically similar sections of a media signal will be marked with a similar watermark. Now our approach is to calculate a sufficient number of individual watermarks suited for a given media section which is then are matched and selected by an audio fingerprint.

The embedding of the watermark with the help of the audio fingerprint is described in the following sections.

3.1   Preprocessing the Lookup Collection

This processing step features fingerprinting and watermark on the media data. It should be noted that the *generic* concept is independent from the actual watermarking algorithm involved. It can be applied with any watermarking algorithm that allows calculating a difference signal between the original cover and a marked audio segment in a suitable data domain in a meaningful way. A typical example for audio data would be the sample-wise difference in the PCM domain between cover and marked segment. We furthermore require that adding such difference signal to *new* media data *other than the initial cover* imprints the watermark in that data, too.

The watermark lookup collection is created using an arbitrarily predefined set of cover audio content, as follows:

a)   At first, the audio content is divided into short sections (less than a second in practice) and each section will provide the payload for one bit of the watermark message. All audio sections are watermarked with both the "one" and the "zero" message symbol. Here, the embedding is controlled by an appropriate psycho-acoustic model and it is dependent on the predefined individual watermark key of the user.

b)   Then, the difference signal between the *watermarked* audio sections and the corresponding *cover* audio sections is calculated, sample-by-sample, in the time-domain and saved to the lookup collection. For later adjustment to the volume of the audio to be watermarked, also the power level ratio of this difference signal relative to the original cover is saved to the lookup collection.

c)   Finally, for each audio section, its audio fingerprint of the cover data is calculated and saved to the lookup collection serving as an index for later access.

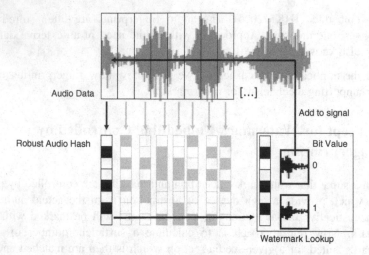

Fig. 1. Embedding concept for audio data. The audio fingerprint (denoted as "Robust Audio Hash") is derived from the audio data. It is matched within watermark lookup collection. Depending on the bit value to be embedded, the watermark signal "0" or "1" is added to the audio data at the position of the corresponding fingerprint.

3.2 Embedding the Watermark Message

Using the lookup collection, an arbitrary audio file is watermarked as follows (see Figure 1):

a) Media parsing: When the user wants to embed a watermark in a media file, he needs the watermark lookup collection as explained before. He first calculates the audio fingerprint of the first section of the media file. The audio fingerprint can be seen as an index to find the best match in the lookup collection of difference signals with respect to similarity of the psycho-acoustic properties.

b) Matching to lookup collection: The audio fingerprint is used to access the watermark lookup collection. The entry with the best match in terms of the Hamming distance is selected. Then, depending on the value of the current watermarking bit to be embedded at the current media file position, the algorithm accesses the pre-generated watermark difference signal for message symbol "1" or "0" in the collection.

c) Watermark embedding: The difference signal retrieved from the watermark lookup collection is added sample-by-sample to the current media data section. As its audio fingerprint is related to the masking curve used to pre-generate the watermark, the transparency of the embedded watermark and therefore the quality of the marked cover is ensured. The volume of the difference signal is adjusted to the volume of the given audio cover based on the power level information which is available in the lookup collection. Although the level dependence in the psycho acoustic model is non-linear, this approach can be seen as a sufficient adaption to the sound pressure level. In fact, closer analysis showed that this volume adjustment could avoid audible distortions caused by difference signals in the lookup collection that were obtained from audio segments with high volume. Additionally, the difference signal can be multiplied with a *global factor* to evaluate different levels of embedding strength.

d) The addition of the watermark can be done with minimal computational effort, e.g. by adding the watermark directly in the time-domain to the media information, avoiding costly spectral transformation during the embedding process and several steps of overlap-adding including fading.

e) Loop: The algorithm proceeds in the sequence of media data sections and embedded additional watermarking bits as described in steps a) to c) as long as there is media data to be marked.

An alternative approach for volume adjustment in step c) could be to use a lookup collection from audio content which was specially prepared in the pre-processing stage (see section 3.1 above): Prior to embedding, one could apply *compression of the dynamics* (difference of volume between loud and silent segments) and amplification of the (now almost constant) volume to a defined value. Then, lookup collections for different volumes could be used to obtain an even better matching.

It must be noted that the pre-processing is done only once for each user and media data type as long as the user's secret key is not changed. The reason an individual collection needs to be generated only once lies within the security requirements. If no key-based security is needed, all users of the algorithm could use the same watermark lookup collection. In that case, pre-processing (step 1) would not be necessary for individual users, but they would access a global pre-generated collection provided together with the algorithm.

4 Implementation of Fingerprint Extraction

This chapter describes the fingerprint extraction we use for psychoacoustic-based matching and for the creation of the lookup-table. It features several content-based analysis methods from the literature, for example, psychoacoustic modeling [ISO1993], MPEG-7 low level audio features [AHHF+2001], audio fingerprinting [HaOK2001] and adaptive quantization as published by us in an earlier work [ZmSt2008].

The calculation requires several processing steps as follows:

- Segmentation of the audio stream: at first, the cover, a PCM audio file is divided in frames of appropriate length, e.g. 512, 1024 or 2048 samples and the FFT spectrum is calculated before further processing frame-by-frame. For synchronizing the watermark embedding and the audio feature extraction, as described in the following, the correspondent frames show no overlap. That is, the fingerprints are extracted from separate audio frames, independently.

- Fingerprinting from psycho-acoustic modeling: Based on the MPEG psychoacoustic model, from the FFT spectrum the instantaneous masking threshold of each frame is calculated [ISO1993]. This is the curve of minimum sound pressure level that is required to add an *additional* sound sensation to the present audio signal. Its calculation is based on models for human perception of sound, namely frequency and temporal masking. It provides an abstracted representation that is nevertheless significant with respect to Human perception of the sound in the audio fragment. Thus, analyzing the masking curve in each time-step is a promising approach to match audio content based on human perception. Here, the signal-to-mask ratio is analyzed and the *psychoacoustic status fingerprint H1* of length N Bit is defined as follows: First, the cover FFT spectrum and the masking curve are divided into N subbands. Then, for each subband, the i-th bit in *H1* is set to "1" (or "0", respectively) if the mean of the given cover FFT spectrum is above (or below, respectively) the mean of the masking threshold in that subband. It should be noted that in practice, while creating the lookup collection, this requires no significant extra computational effort as the psycho acoustic modeling needs and the FFT spectrum need to be available for the embedding, anyway.

- Fingerprinting from adaptively quantized spectrum: As an intermediate processing step, the FFT spectrum is quantized depending on *H1*: Inaudible areas, i.e. those parts in the spectrum which are below the masking threshold, are represented coarsely with 1-bit quantization. Audible areas above the masking threshold are represented up to 7-bit quantization. As shown in [ZmSt2008] this increases the robustness of the following fingerprint extraction because acoustically irrelevant signal changes will contribute less to the result or will be even ignored. Then we compare the spectral coefficients in two consecutive time-steps among the N subbands according to the audio fingerprinting approach presented in [HaOK2001]. We define the *frequency frame fingerprint H2* as follows: we assign a "1" if the mean of the coefficients increases from first to second time step, and vice versa.

- Fingerprinting from spectrum flatness analysis: Another feature used is the *spectrum flatness* calculated from the N subbands in two consecutive frames. The flatness measure is defined as the ratio between the geometric and arithmetic mean of the spectral coefficients [AHHF+2001]. Spectrum flatness is a measure that indicates if a spectrum or subband contains dominant peaks or if the spectrum is rather "flat". Thus, it can identify, if a certain audio spectrum contains dominant single tones or not. Calculated among a number of subbands, it can be seen as another approach to identify similar audio content [AHHF+2001]. From the flatness measure, the *spectrum flatness fingerprint H3* of length N Bit is defined similar to *H1* by comparing the flatness values between two adjacent time steps among all subbands similar to [HaKa2001, HaOK2001].

5   Experimental Evaluation

To evaluate the performance of the proposed scheme, we performed tests on synthetic and real-world audios of different genre. Here, the suitability of the proposed fingerprinting algorithms, the sound quality and the overall watermark detection success were of special interest.

5.1 Test Set and Creation of Lookup Collection

We created a lookup collection using different fingerprinting schemes *H1*, *H2* and *H3* and different combinations thereof, respectively. The fingerprints were of 12 bit length. The lookup collection was created from a 261 seconds rock music audio file. Here, a spread-spectrum Patchwork [BGML1996] watermarking approach from our earlier work [Stei2003] was used. That audio watermarking approach features an embedding and detection in the Fourier domain while the transparency is maintained by a psycho acoustic model similar to the model used in lossy encoding of *mp2* and *mp3* files [ISO1993]. The difference signals between the cover audio and the temporary watermarked copies with message symbols "0" and "1" were obtained from the PCM audio data in the time-domain.

5.2 Comparison of Different Fingerprint Approaches

To give a proof that suitable pre-watermarked audio segments can be recognized using fingerprinting, several audio files from several genre (pop, rock, movie score, synthetic white noise) of 773 seconds total length were used for later embedding. In total, 75 watermark messages of 8 bit net length (approx. ten seconds play time per message) were embedded using our proposed approach. A CRC-12 checksum was appended to every watermark message to be able to verify the integrity of arbitrary messages at detection time. That message of length 8+12=20 Bit was subject to forward error correction (FEC). We use a convolutional encoding / Viterbi decoding to improve the robustness and to cope with bit errors during transmission. The FEC encoding increases the message length, again, to a gross length of 2*20+4=44 Bit total. To increase the robustness, each bit was embedded several times in consecutive frames.

Every message was prefixed by a *synchronization* template of 40 bit, i.e. approximately two seconds. That is, before the beginning of any arbitrary watermark message, a *static* watermark message pattern is embedded that is fixed and known for any message. This enables the watermark detector to synchronize to the precise embedding position and allows watermark detection even when the audio files were trimmed.

Global factors of 1.0 and 2.0 were used for embedding. A factor greater that one means that the selected difference signal will be added to the new cover data with a higher volume than it was originally present when the lookup collection was created.

For further analysis, the three fingerprints are combined with the XOR operation. That allows providing a combined fingerprint to which all three individual fingerprinting schemes contribute while maintaining its total bit length. Seven different combinations of hashes are performed, namely the three individual hashes and all XOR combinations thereof.

We finally obtain an *N* Bit audio fingerprint which we will use for matching the audio content to the appropriate lookup collection entry. In practice, fingerprint lengths *N* from 10 to 12 are used in order to keep the size of the lookup collection compact.

The detection results are obtained without any attacks applied to the watermarked content. From the detection results given in Table 1 the following can be seen:

- The overall detection success is rather moderate as 47% of the embedded messages can be retrieved at best (35 out of 75 for global factor of 2.0 when *H1+H3* is used).
- It can be seen that a global factor of 2.0 during embedding provides much more detected watermark messages compared to a global factor of 1.0 (total 152 instead of 71), as can be expected.
- It is obvious that fingerprint *H3* outperforms the other two fingerprints when a *single* fingerprint is used: almost no message was detected when only *H1* or only *H2* was used.
- Surprisingly, an XOR combination *H1* with *H2* again provided a significant number of successful detections while they individually provide poor results.

Closer analysis showed that many of the incorrectly retrieved messages were actually almost correct but *one* the eight bits. Closer look at the single message bits showed that the bit error rate was at best 0.192 for fingerprint H3 and global factor of 2x and detection threshold of 0.2. That explains why only 31 out of 75 messages could be successfully *and* completely decoded in the Viterbi decoder, in that best case.

Table 1. Correctly detected watermark messages; the "+" symbol denotes XOR operation

		H1	**H2**	**H3**	**H1+H2**	**H1+H3**	**H2+H3**	**H1+H2+H3**	**Total**
global factor	**1.0**	0	0	23	6	12	21	9	**71**
	2.0	1	0	31	33	35	26	26	**152**

fingerprint combination used

Table 2. Correctly detected sync templates; the "+" symbol denotes XOR operation

		H1	**H2**	**H3**	**H1+H2**	**H1+H3**	**H2+H3**	**H1+H2+H3**	**Total**
global factor	**1.0**	4	2	35	38	32	47	31	**189**
	2.0	0	0	59	66	58	55	48	**286**

fingerprint combination used

Thus, to verify if it is plausible to use even shorter message lengths, we also analyzed, how many of the synchronization templates (only two seconds each) can be detected correctly From Table 2 we can see that, indeed, the detection success for the sync templates is two to three times higher than for the full watermark message payload. That is, shorter watermark messages (or splitting the watermarking message, resp.) will be useful. Again, fingerprint *H3* outperforms all other approaches by far, if single algorithms are compared.

5.3   Assessment of Sound Quality

We also analyzed the sound quality of embedded audio. For this purpose, the embedded and original audios were compared using the *OPERA Audio Quality Analysis*[3] system. In contrast to *simple* quality measures like PSNR, it simulates and considers Human perception of sound. It features an artificial neural network which simulates Human perception of quality degradation as perceived by an average listener. The artificial neural network was trained with large sets of listening tests during the development of the lossy mp3 audio compression. The *OPERA* system allows efficient and reproducible comparison of audio data before and after processing while avoiding elaborate listening tests.

The sound quality is expressed in terms of the *Objective Difference Grade (ODG)* which ranges from 0.0 (*"no audible difference"*) to -4.0 (*"very annoying"*), see definition in Table 3. For example, closer analysis shows that the quality loss caused by mp3 encoding of typical music files at 128kBit/s, stereo, is assessed with approximately -1.0 on the ODG scale, which is according to common user acceptance.

Table 3. Definition of Objective Difference Grades

ODG	Sound sensation
0	no audible difference
-1	slightly different, not annoying
-2	little annoying
-3	annoying
-4	very annoying

The plot of number of successful detections versus the sound quality loss under different global factor values is expressed in Figures 2a and 2b: For a low embedding strength (global factor 1.0) it can be see that the results on the sound quality are clearly divided: most of the marked files feature ODG values between -0.5 and 0.0 which means that the distortions introduced by our embedding approach are almost inaudible. Unfortunately, only a few watermark messages could be detected in that case, no matter which fingerprinting strategy was used. On the opposite, there are a few samples that feature a large number of correct detections. But they suffer from an extremely low ODG near -4.0 which indicates very annoying distortions.

The results look more promising if a higher embedding strength is selected (see Figure 2b). For global factor of 2.0 a number of test runs showed successful detections greater than zero while the ODG values remains greater than -1.0, i.e. the sound quality is not annoyingly distorted.

The detailed results for a selection of individual files for fingerprint H3 are given in Table 4. There, it can be seen again, how the results are dependent on the different files. For example, the "Rock1" music song ("Black Ice" by AC/DC) could be

---

[3] www.opticom.de (URL verified January 2012).

watermarked with 1 to 8 messages. But the sound quality was very poor, no matter which global factor (embedding strength) was used. For the "Rock2" song ("I'll give you money (live)" by Peter Frampton), at least four messages could be detected correctly while the sound quality loss was "slightly annoying".

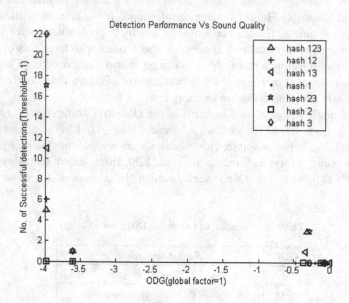

Fig. 2a. Detection success and quality loss for different audio files and different strategies of fingerprints (denoted as "hash"); global factor = 1.0

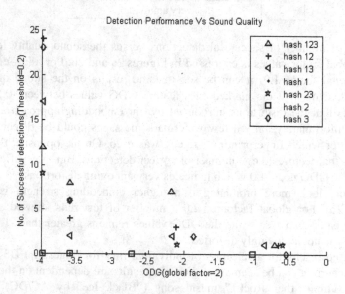

Fig. 2b. Detection success and quality loss for different audio files and different strategies of fingerprints ("hash"); global factor = 2.0

Table 4. Results on detection and sound quality among different files

File Name	ODG		Number of detections	
	Global factor 1.0	Global factor 2.0	Global factor 1.0	Global factor 2.0
Rock1	-3.60	-3.60	1	8
Movie Score	-3.98	-3.98	22	19
Rock2	-0.27	-1.87	0	4
Noise	-0.06	-0.55	0	0

5.4   Distribution of Fingerprints

We further investigated, why the results were so different among different files. One reason might be that the lookup collection we used was created from only one music file (i.e. one musical genre) of a few minutes play length. From Figure 3 we can see that most of the possible 4096 values of the 12-bit fingerprint actually were not used. Closer analysis showed that during embedding, the best matches still have a Hamming distance significantly greater than zero, i.e. *exact* matches were very rare.

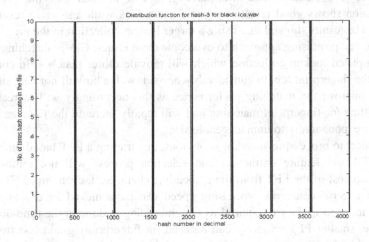

Fig. 3. Distribution of the 2^{12} possible fingerprint values; Lookup collection obtained from a 261 second rock music song

One solution is to create a larger lookup collection in the preparation stage. First test results from a 30 minute test file containing different kinds of musical genre and speech data showed a distribution that is much less sparse (see Figure 4). Closer analysis showed that only approximately 100 out of 4096 possible fingerprint values were missing in the lookup collection displayed in Figure 4.

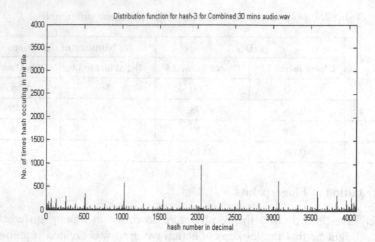

Fig. 4. Distribution of the 2^{12} possible fingerprint values; Lookup collection obtained from a 30 minutes music compilation

5.5   Discussion of Results

With respect to robustness and transparency, it can be said that the proposed implementation shows good results for some audio files while moderate results for other files. The results showed that using a larger lookup collection in the preparation stage can be one promising approach to overcome these issues: Closer matching using a more completed lookup collection which will provide closer matches. In contrast, increasing the fingerprint length considerably beyond twelve bit will not be a suitable solution to improve the matching performance as this accordingly will increase the processing time for fingerprint matching and will rapidly increase the file size of the lookup table exponentially to unmanageable size.

With respect to processing speed, it is obvious, that trading a FFT-based embedder with a FFT-based feature extraction and selection process will not remove the computational cost of the FFT from the embedding chain. Still, even with FFT-based fingerprints a certain gain in processing speed can be achieved in our approach because no inverted FFTs are required as the embedding is done in the time-domain. Furthermore, smaller FFT windows can be used for fingerprinting and less overlap-adding is required.

For example, given by the implementation that was used for the experimental section [Stei2006], the embedding of each message bit in a frame requires several internal steps of FFT and inverted FFT calculation (frame size 2048 samples), fading and overlap-adding to obtain optimal transparency. Instead, the proposed approach requires one FFT of frame size 1024 for fingerprinting-based matching plus adding in the time-domain the 2048 samples difference signal to the cover audio.

In summary, it must be said that the fingerprinting methods applied above are only current examples used to implement a *proof of concept*. Nevertheless, the above implementation, in which fingerprinting controls the embedding process, shows to be an alternative embedding strategy *in principle*.

6   Summary and Outlook

In this work we present a concept and its proof for efficient embedding of digital watermarks in audio data. It is based on creating a *lookup collection* of watermarking difference signals and corresponding audio fingerprints from an arbitrary set of audio files during a pre-processing step. Here, the Fingerprints are used as a supporting audio pattern recognition mechanism to increase the processing speed of digital watermarking.

When a media file is to be watermarked, its audio frames are matched against the lookup collection. Here, an audio fingerprint is calculated for each frame and used for audio pattern recognition. Only the pre-processed watermark message bit with the best match with respect to perceptual properties is taken from the lookup collection. This watermark is then added to the signal by simply mixing both signals. Then, the algorithm proceeds to the next frame and so on. That is, the lookup collection can be used at any later date with arbitrary PCM files to create watermarked at very high processing speed and low computational effort.

It should be noted that the concept is independent from the media type of audio data as discussed here. The concept of perceptual matching can be applied to image or video watermarking, for example, as visual models provide an assessment of perceptual similarity of visual content.

In extension to our previous conceptual work, here, real-world test results proof that the concept is performing successfully *in principle*. Approximately one half of the embedded watermark can be retrieved under optimal conditions. Nevertheless, the results for sound quality show room for improvement before applying the approach for real-world applications. Using larger lookup collections or introducing different volume adjustment seems to be promising approaches for improving the transparency and/or robustness of the embedding.

In our future work, further fingerprinting approaches shall be investigated that provide a better match in terms of acoustic similarity and watermark transparency. To improve the computational costs, one focus will be on extracting fingerprints in the time-domain for avoiding time-consuming spectral transformation in the future.

We will also proof that this approach can enable a *fast* embedding. Therefore, the current MATLAB implementation will be ported to Java or C/C++ and compared to current audio watermarking solutions with respect to computational costs.

Acknowledgement. This work has been supported by the Center of Advanced Security Research Darmstadt (*CASED*), funded by the German federal state of Hesse under the LOEWE programme (http://www.cased.de).

References

[AHHF+2001]   Allamanche, E., Herre, J., Helmuth, O., Frba, B., Kasten, T., Cremer, M.: Content-Based Identification of Audio Material Using MPEG-7 Low Level Description. In: Proc. of 2nd International Symposium of Music Information Retrieval (ISMIR 2001), Indiana University, Bloomington, Indiana, USA, October 15-17 (2001),
http://ismir2001.ismir.net/proceedings.html
(URL verified: January 2012)

[BGML1996]   Bender, W., Gruhl, D., Morimoto, N., Lu, A.: Techniques for data hiding. IBM Systems Journal 35(3,4), 313–336 (1996)

[CMB2002]   Cox, I.J., Miller, M.L., Bloom, J.A.: Digital Watermarking. Academic Press, San Diego (2002) ISBN 1-55860-714-5

[FG2000]   Fridrich, J., Goljan, M.: Robust Hash Functions for Digital Watermarking. In: International Symposium on Information Technology (ITCC 2000), March 27-29. IEEE Computer Society, Las Vegas (2000) ISBN 0-7695-0540-6

[HaKa2001]   Haitsma, J.A., Kalker, T.: A highly robust audio fingerprinting system. In: 2nd International Symposium of Music Information Retrieval (ISMIR 2001), Bloomington, Indiana, USA (2001), Online proceeding,
http://ismir2001.ismir.net/proceedings.html
(link verified: July 07, 2011)

[HaOK2001]   Haitsma, J., Oostveen, J., Kalker, T.: Robust Audio Hashing for Content Identification. In: Proc. of Content-based Multimedia Indexing (CBMI 2001), Brescia, Italy (2001)

[HBS2007]   Hauer, E., Bölke, T., Steinebach, M.: Framework for combined video frame synchronization and watermark detection. In: Delp III, E.J., Wong, P.W. (eds.) Security, Steganography, and Watermarking of Multimedia Contents IX. SPIE / IS&T, Bellingham (2007) ISBN: 9780819466181

[HKM2005]   Harmanci, O., Kucukgoz, M., Mihcak, M.: Temporal synchronization of watermarked video using image hashing. In: Proc. of IEEE Security, Steganography and Watermarking of Multimedia Contents VII, San Jose, USA, vol. 5681, pp. 370–380 (January 2005)

[ISO1993]   ISO/IEC 11172-3, MPEG-1: Coding of moving pictures and associated audio for digital storage media at up to about 1.5 MBit/s, Part 3:Audio (1993)

[KCLI+2007]   Kirbiz, S., Celik, M., Lemma, A., Katzenbeisser, S.: Decode-Time Forensic Watermarking of AAC Bit-Streams. IEEE Transactions on Information Forensics and Security 2(4), 683–696 (2007)

[OST1994]   Osborne, C.F., van Schyndel, R.G., Tirkel, A.Z.: A Digital Watermark. In: IEEE International Conference on Image Processing, Austin, Texas, pp. 86–90 (November 1994)

[SHW2007]   Steinebach, M., Hauer, E., Wolf, P.: Efficient Watermarking Strategies. In: Third International Conference on Automated Production of Cross Media Content for Multi-Channel Distribution (AXMEDIS 2007), pp. 65–71 (2007)

[Stei2003]   Steinebach, M.: Digitale Wasserzeichen für Audiodaten. Shaker Verlag Aachen (2003) ISBN 3832225072

[SZF2006]   Steinebach, M., Zmudzinski, S., Fan, C.: The digital watermarking container: Secure and efficient embedding. In: Proceedings of the ACM Multimedia and Security Workshop, Magdeburg, Germany, September 20-21 (2004)

[SZN2006]   Steinebach, M., Zmdzinski, S., Neichtadt, S.: Robust-audio-hash Synchronized Audio Watermarking. In: Paphos, C., Fernández-Medina, E., Yagüe, M.I. (eds.) 4th International Workshop on Security in Information Systems (WOSIS 2006), pp. S.58–S.66 (2006)

[WHS2008]   Wolf, P., Hauer, E., Steinebach, M.: The video watermarking container: efficient realtime transaction watermarking. In: Delp, Wong, Dittmann, Memon (eds.) Proceeding of Electronic Imaging 2008: Security, Steganography, and Watermarking of Multimedia Contents X. SPIE IS&T, Bellingham (2008) ISBN: 978-08194-6995-3

[ZmSt2008]   Zmudzinski, S., Steinebach, M.: Robust audio hashing for audio authentication watermarking. In: Delp, Wong, Dittmann, Memon (eds.) Proceeding of Electronic Imaging 2008: Security, Steganography, and Watermarking of Multimedia Contents X (2008) ISBN: 978-08194-6995-3

Plausibility Considerations on Steganalysis as a Security Mechanism – Discussions on the Example of Audio Steganalysis

Christian Kraetzer and Jana Dittmann

Otto-von-Guericke-University Magdeburg, Dept. of Computer Science,
Research Group Multimedia and Security
P.O. Box 4120, 39016 Magdeburg, Germany
{kraetzer,dittmann}@iti.cs.uni-magdeburg.de

Abstract. Most publications on steganography and steganalysis trivialize the latter into a simple two-class decision problem: either a data object is an unmodified cover or a stego object. The normal way in literature to tackle this decision problem is to use supervised classification, first, to train classifiers and, second, to compute the classification accuracies on known good (cover) and known bad (stego) samples in artificially constructed evaluation sets with known classes for all objects. It is true that such statistical pattern recognition (SPR) based approaches might be efficient for solving the steganalysis problem, but in practical application it is less trivial and to achieve plausible results is much harder. The scientific contribution of this paper is to address the lack in investigation methodologies and metrics for steganalysis benchmarking and plausibility considerations. We consider the state-of-the-art in this field and enhance it by new considerations on steganalyser throughput and plausibility. The work presented here includes a recommendation for an advanced metric to measure the throughput of a steganalyser.

Keywords: Steganalysis as a security service, audio steganalysis, throughput, plausibility.

1   Motivation and Introduction

Steganalysis, as the technique to detect hidden communication channels in media files or streams, is one of a number of important techniques to establish trust in media data. The most common solution used to implement steganalysis to detect steganography by cover modification is statistical pattern recognition (SPR).

A first interesting point to be mentioned in the context of this paper is the mismatch between research and development/application in the field of steganalysis. For other communication based threat scenarios in IT-security, like viruses/malware or email spam, a large range of commercial detectors is available. But in steganalysis, it contrast to the hundreds or even thousands of research publications focussing on this topic, only few open source or research demonstrator steganalysers are found

Y.Q. Shi (Ed.): Transactions on DHMS VIII, LNCS 7228, pp. 80–101, 2012.

together with an even smaller number of commercial steganalysis detectors. Also, for those few commercial tools available the focus of application is in many cases not statistical analysis of potential cover objects[1].

Most publications on steganography and steganalysis trivialize the latter into a simple two-class decision problem: either a data object is an unmodified cover or a stego object. The normal way in literature to tackle this decision problem is to use supervised classification, first, to train classifiers and, second, to compute the classification accuracies on known good (cover) and known bad (stego) samples in artificially constructed evaluation sets with known classes for all objects. It is true that such statistical pattern recognition (SPR) based approaches might be efficient for solving the steganalysis problem, but in practical application it is less trivial and to achieve plausible results is much harder.

Kodovský and Fridrich conclude in [14] that there are three main factors that can negatively influence the performance of machine learning tools: small number of training samples, low class distinguishability and high dimensionality of the feature space. They declare that weak steganographic methods are easily detectable because they disturb some elementary cover properties that can be captured by a low-dimensional feature vector with high distinguishability. A fairly small training dataset is then usually sufficient to train a classifier with an excellent performance. While on the other hand, more advanced steganographic methods require high-dimensional feature spaces capable of capturing more complex dependencies among individual cover elements, which in turn necessitates more training samples. A seemingly straightforward strategy to improve the performance of existing steganalysers may be to increase the size of the training set. This way we allow the machine learning tool to better utilise the given feature space and we may use feature spaces of higher dimensions without degradation of performance. However, sooner or later one will likely encounter technical problems with data or memory management, or the training would be unacceptably long. Furthermore, in many practical scenarios, the steganalyst lacks information about the cover source (only a limited number of cover examples are available). Here, training the classifier on a different cover source may result in a serious drop in testing performance (see e.g. [7], [8]).

The main points of the statements from Kodovský and Fridrich can be restated as: statistical relevance (with an implicit threat of overfitting), class distinguishability, curse of high dimensionality (complexity) and missing context information problems. From a scientific point of view this list is identifying the major problems known in pattern recognition research since decades. Nevertheless, we want to show that those considerations in [14] are far from being complete – especially if it is intended to implement a steganalyser as a field-deployable security mechanism (like e.g. an anti-malware scanner, an intrusion detection system or a firewall).

This paper summarises and extends the considerations found in [14] as well as our previous considerations from [24], [3] and [27] on audio steganalysis, by addressing

---

[1] The SARC steganalyser (see http://www.sarc-wv.com/products/stegalyzeras/learn_more.aspx) claims to detect the download and installation of over 925 steganography applications on MS Windows machines.

the following six important aspects on the plausibility of practically applied steganalysis:

a)   considering the detection performance (or classification accuracy) of the steganalysers as initial/naïve trust assumption

b)   the differentiation between the different error classes encountered (i.e. if steganalysis is considered a two-class classification problem then between the statistical Type I and Type II errors – false positives and false negatives)

c)   the statistical generalisability of the results at hand considering known problems from classification (like overfitting) and required evaluation set sizes – this includes considerations on the correlation between the training context and the application context (i.e. context dependent and independent training and testing)

d)   the influence of other (non-malicious) audio signal processing operations on the steganalyser has to be investigated

e)   the plausibility of the features used for classification actually being relevant for the classification problem at hand

f)   the possibilities for increasing and estimating the decision performance in case of information fusion by multiple steganalysers

For a security mechanism that aims at the detection of malicious behaviour (here the construction of hidden communication channels) the question of the **throughput** and/or detector response time are imminent. In the field application of a steganalysis performing security mechanism, the preferred throughput would obviously be a real-time system with a very short detector response time, which would allow for the implementation of detection and prevention systems. Nevertheless, it is hard to generalize the real-time requirements because the cover channels can be of different nature: they could be rather low data-rate audio-based communication channels (e.g. GSM, VoIP, radio broadcasts) or high data-rate audio material transmitted via data transfer protocols (e.g. MP3 files via file sharing networks). Furthermore, all publicly available / known audio steganalysis tools (which would form the core of a steganalysis security mechanism) are right now rather slow, due to the complex analysis task at hand (see section 2). Nevertheless, a methodology and designs for the throughput analysis for steganalysers are required in this field, for performance evaluations on single steganalysis algorithms as well as for complex fusion information systems combining multiple steganalysers.

Next to the throughput, another important point is the **plausibility of decisions** made by a steganalysis performing security mechanism. The notion of plausibility used within this paper combines different aspects: first, the initial detection performance (or classification accuracy) of the steganalysers, second, the differentiation between the different error classes encountered (i.e. if steganalysis is considered a two-class classification problem then between the statistical Type I and Type II errors – false positives and false negatives), third, the statistical generalisability of the results at hand considering known problems from classification, required evaluation set sizes and the correlation between the training context and the application context has to be considered (i.e. context dependent and independent training and testing), fourth, the influence of other (non-malicious) audio signal processing operations on the steganalyser has to be investigated, fifth, the plausibility of the features used for classification actually being relevant for the classification problem at hand, and sixth, the possibilities for increasing and estimating the decision performance in case of information fusion by multiple steganalysers.

If a steganalysis performing security mechanism detects the presence of hidden channels in the cover data under observation, further **information to characterize the steganographic channel** might be derived from by the detector, including the used embedding domain and an algorithm identification, key scenario considerations as well as payload estimation.

In some scenarios it might be possible to apply **countermeasures** in case a steganographic channel is detected. In the simplest case, the countermeasure might be a disruption of the cover channel. More sophisticated measures might be found in filtering operations on the cover data to eliminate the embedded steganographic information without disrupting the entire cover channel.

The scientific contribution of this paper is to address the lack in investigation methodologies and metrics for steganalysis benchmarking. We consider the state-of-the-art in this field and enhance it by new considerations on steganalyser throughput and plausibility. The work presented here includes a recommendation for an advanced metric to measure the throughput of a steganalyser.

The rest of this paper is structured as follows: section 2 summarises briefly the state-of-the-art in the fields of plausibility considerations in steganalysis and on steganalyser benchmarking, section 3 introduces our methodologies, concepts and new metrics for practical steganalysis. In section 4 the benefit of the application of our methodology and concepts in practice is demonstrated briefly. Section 5 summarises the paper and discusses perspectives for future work.

2   State-of-the-Art in Plausibility Considerations for Steganalysis and in Steganalyser Benchmarking

One of the rare examples where steganalysis is applied in large scale field evaluations is the work of Niels Provos and Peter Honeyman in [16]. In their paper, the authors criticise current state-of-the-art in steganalytical approaches at this point of time (like [18] and [19]) as being practically infeasible, due to faulty basic assumptions (two-class problem description and statistical overfitting to the training sets). In contrast to these publications Provos and Honeyman construct a multi-class SPR-based image steganalysis detector called Stegdetect. Each candidate image is considered to be member of one of four classes, either it is an unmodified cover image or it is the result of the application of one out of three different steganographic tools (JSteg, JPHide and OutGuess 0.13b) which have been amongst the state-of-the-art at this point of time. Stegdetect is then applied blindly (without knowledge about the true class) to two million images downloaded from eBay auctions and one million images obtained from USENET archives. As a result, Stegdetect implies that over 1%

of all images seem to have been steganographically altered (mostly by JPHide) and therefore contain hidden messages. Based on these findings, Provos and Honeyman describe in [16] also a second tool called Stegbreak for plausibility considerations, i.e. for verifying the existence of messages hidden by JPHide in the images identified by Stegdetect. Their verification approach is based on the assumption that at least some of the passwords used as embedding key for the steganographic embedding are weak passwords[2]. Based on this assumption, they implement for Stegbreak a dictionary attack using JPHide's retrieval function and large (about 1,800,000 words) multi-language dictionaries. This attack is applied to all images that have been flagged as stego-objects by the statistical analyses in Stegdetect.

To verify the correctness of their tools, Provos and Honeyman insert tracer images into every Stegbreak job. As expected the dictionary attack finds the correct passwords for these tracer images. However, they do not find any single genuine hidden message. In their paper, they offer four possible interpretations of this result, either: a) there is no significant use of steganography on the internet, b) they have been analyzing images from sources that are not used to carry steganographic content, c) nobody uses steganographic systems that we can find, or d) all users of steganographic systems carefully choose passwords that are not susceptible to dictionary attacks. Even though the result of this large scale investigation is negative, the methodology and concepts behind the work in [16] are remarkable. Even more so, since they also perform throughput considerations (throughput for Stegdetect is given in Kilobit of images per seconds; the throughput for Stegbreak is given in words per second for the dictionary attack) for their analysis tool-chain, something that is also strongly amiss in most steganalysis publications.

While, as mentioned above, most scientific publications trivialize steganalysis into a simple two-class decision problem and focus on reporting classification accuracies for supervised classification obtained under certain evaluation setups, some authors include considerations that aim directly or indirectly at the verification of the plausibility of the their detection approaches. A good example for this class of publications is [22]. In this paper the authors perform a feature selection in a SPR-based steganalysis approach to reduce the complexity of the classification task.

A completely different view on the plausibility of stenography and steganalysis is presented in [20]. In this document instructions are given for potential end-users how to evaluate the actual security of existing steganographic tools. Following the instructions it is simple to identify all tools that are not compliant with Kerckhoffs principle [21]. Furthermore, basic statistical techniques are explained that allow estimating the statistical impact of steganography by modification for steganographic tools. Also, the influence of strong encryption prior to embedding and other basic considerations are discussed.

Summarising the state-of-the-art in plausibility considerations in steganalysis and steganalyser benchmarking, it has to be said that most of the work found in literature so far is limited to investigations on the performance against individual steganographic algorithms, not on considerations as a global security mechanism that

---

[2] A study conducted by Klein found nearly 25% of all passwords are weak passwords [17].

could be implemented and applied as a tool like e.g. a malware scanner. Especially the lack of appropriate metrics, as required for sophisticated performance evaluation and steganalysis benchmarking, is a strong problem for this domain. So far the most often found concept for classifier/detector comparison in this field is the usage of the classification accuracy as the one and only metric for performance estimations. Many publications consider a steganalysis algorithm to be better than another one simply if its classification accuracy on the same test set is higher. Such a statement is not taking the whole complexity of the steganalysis problem into account. Important further considerations, like the throughput of the detector, the distribution of error classes (Type I errors or False Positives vs. Type II error or False Negatives), etc are most often completely neglected.

3 Methodologies, Concepts and Metrics for Practical Steganalysis

The open research problem identified in section 2, the lack of appropriate metrics for the evaluation of the performance of a steganalysis detector to be implemented into real world application scenarios, is addressed in this section. Here, in section 3.1, first a metric for a throughput analysis for a steganographic detector is discussed because such a cost function would be a necessary condition or sine qua non for every possible field application. Second, trustworthy decisions in an SPR-based steganalysis setup also have to fulfil the plausibility requirements identified in section 1 as sufficient conditions. These are discussed in detail in section 3.2. Sections 3.3 and 3.4 address, very briefly and just for the sake of completeness, two further topics that would have to be considered prior to field application of a steganalysis system. These two topics, which are outside the primary focus of this paper, are: Detector-based steganographic channel characterisation in section 3.3 and the role of countermeasures (i.e. modifications on the cover channel) in section 3.4.

3.1 Throughput Analysis – Runtime and Accuracy Considerations

In the field-application of a steganalysis-performing security mechanism the preferred throughput would obviously be a reliable (in terms of detector accuracy) real-time system with a very short detector response time. This would allow, in the application domain chosen here, for the implementation of detection and prevention systems observing audio communication channels or audio file transfers. To our knowledge, all currently publicly available audio steganalysis tools (which would form the core of a steganalysis security mechanism) are far from being close to this preferred throughput, due to the complex analysis task at hand (see section 2.). Nevertheless, a methodology and concepts to allow for the throughput analysis for steganalysers are required in this field, for performance evaluations on single steganalysis algorithms as well as for complex fusion information systems combining multiple steganalysers.

We introduce an initial methodology for such a throughput analysis in [27] where we compare the performance of three selected information hiding (IH) algorithms. The introduced concept models this problem as the gain to cost ratio between detection performance (as gain) and run-time required (run-time complexity as cost). The initial design used in [27] expresses this ratio for a classical two-class consideration on the steganalysis problem as shown in equation 1.

$$q = \begin{cases} \dfrac{accuracy}{runtime} & if \quad accuracy > 50\% \\ 0 & if \quad accuracy = 50\% \end{cases} \tag{1}$$

If the accuracy (the ratio between true classifications and all classification attempts in a supervised classification) of the classifier used for steganalysis is better than guessing (i.e. 50% in this two-class problem), then its classifier throughput performance q is determined by the *accuracy* achieved on a fixed sized classification problem divided by the classifiers *runtime* (combined training and testing times) on this problem for a selected test computer. The measurement unit of this computation would be percentage of true (positive and negative) classifications per second, which is, for the standardised set sizes used here, a simplified version of the more intuitive "percentage of correctly classified files per second" ratio. The results presented in [27] for an analysis of 74 single classifiers show that this concept can indeed be used to distinguish between suitable and unsuitable classifiers based on the computed throughput performance.

Nevertheless, it has to be admitted that this simple analysis concept is unfair and its result hard to interpret. From a scientific point it is unfair, because it does not compare the classification algorithms but instead compares their implementations. Therefore, a rather well suited algorithm implemented in an interpreted language might be ranked lower than a less suitable algorithm implemented directly in machine code, only because the latter can be executed much faster. For the same reason, results achieved on different computers would not be directly comparable. From the practical point of view these two points, which would be considered as unfair by scientists, would be a desired characteristic of the detection system. The person wanting to install a steganographic channel detector to observe communications or data exchanges would exactly look for the fastest implementation as well as the most suitable (in most cases the fastest) computer to run the detector.

Another point, which makes this concept not exactly unfair but instead inept to handle certain benchmarking problems, is the fact that the accuracy, if used directly, is not suitable for comparisons between different classification problem classes. For example the direct comparison of the classification performance in a two-class classification problem (i.e. the classical hypothesis testing for a assumable steganographically modified channel) and a 4-class problem (e.g. steganographic algorithm identification on a set of three algorithms (plus unmodified covers) that might have been applied, see e.g. the work of Provos and Honeyman summarised in section 2.) would lead to completely misleading results, because in the two-class problem the probability of guessing correctly is two times higher (i.e. 50%, while in the 4-class problem an accuracy of 50% would already be a rather good indicator, being 25% away from the probability of guessing correctly in this case). This point basically implies a strong need for normalization of results.

For the interpretability of the results, the accuracy is expressed as a percentage between 0 and 100% and the runtime is given in seconds and is not bounded. Therefore the result is not normalized in any way so that the actual distance from an "optimal" performance is hard to figure out. Also, the notion of the runtime used here combines the training and the testing times (while in a field application the models would be in many cases assumed to have been trained in advance) of a classifier. Since the ratio between training and testing times varies strongly between individual classifiers, the usage of this combined time might be enormously unfair for application scenarios where the classifier can be trained in advance, i.e. where the characteristics of the expected cover objects and steganographic embedding techniques are known a priori and appropriate training material can be supplied for training. In other application scenarios, where the models could not be trained in advance (due to a lack of knowledge regarding the cover material and/or techniques to be expected or if appropriate training material is missing – see e.g. [4] where the "unmarked" version of an audio file is estimated/predicted by using de-noising on the assumed stego object), this modelling of the runtime would be the only suitable approach.

The points mentioned above led to a redesign of our quality function for the throughput analysis. In the modified version we still use for the runtime the real time required for the classifier (because the ultimate goal would be the practical application in tools and in this case a faster implementation of an algorithm is better than a slower implementation) additionally we introduce a fixed timeout boundary, after which a classifier working on a problem is automatically considered unfit for this problem independent of the classification accuracy he might have achieved in the end. This timeout serves two purposes: first, it makes practical evaluations more feasible by faster removing candidates which would in any case unsuitable for practical application, and second, it allows to generate a normalised runtime description.

$$time = \frac{runtime}{timeout} \qquad (2)$$

Equation 2 shows the normalised runtime description used for an improvement of the quality function for the throughput analysis. The *runtime* is the execution time of the classifier on a given classification problem (training and testing) measured in seconds (using the UNIX time() command [31]). The *timeout* is the timeout-boundary predefined for this investigation. Since the execution of the classifier is terminated at *timeout*, the resulting *time* is a unit-less variable in the range [0,1].

For the accuracy investigations on a classifier, we assume for the further considerations that the *accuracy* (the ratio between the number of all true classifications and all classifications in an test) is expressed in the range of [0,1] instead of a percentage. For n equally distributed classes the probability of guessing correctly is: $probGuess = 1/n$. For not equally distributed classes the probability of guessing correctly has to reflect the ratios between the classes' individual probabilities. To simplify the considerations here, we assume that all training sets for the evaluations are build with equally distributed classes. With the *accuracy* and *probGuess* we can construct for classification-based investigations a degree of closeness of measurements of a quantity to its actual (true) value that is exempt from the influence of the probability of guessing correctly. Such a metric would allow for direct comparison between the classification performances of classifiers on problems of different classes (e.g. a two-class classification problem like the classical hypothesis testing for an assumable steganographically modified channel and a four-class problem like steganographic algorithm identification on a set of three algorithms (plus unmarked covers) that might have been applied).

$$cg = \frac{1}{1 - probGuess}(accuracy - probGuess) \tag{3}$$

Equation 3 gives the metric cg to be used within this paper for the closeness of measurements of a quantity to its true value. It is basically a single-rater version of Cohen's Kappa (see [33], [34] for multi-rater considerations and [35] for single-rater considerations derived from Cohen's Kappa) in the range [0,1]. To construct our new quality metric for the throughput analysis q_{new} we compute the (normalised) Euclidean distance between *time* and an inverted cg. This inversion has to be performed since the *time*, as introduced in equation 2, is a "the-bigger-the-worse" metric and the cg would be a "the-bigger-the-better" metric. The metric q_{new} would therefore be computed as:

$$q_{new} = \frac{1}{\sqrt{2}} \sqrt{time^2 + (1 - cg)^2} \tag{4}$$

Since *time* and cg are bounded in the range [0,1] the Euclidean distance has to be normalised with the square root of 2. The result of this computation q_{new} is, like *time*, a "bigger-the-worse" metric in the range [0,1]. It describes the distance of a current performance from the "optimal" point, which would be a decision machine that gives a perfect classification ($cg=1$) in an extremely short time-span ($time=0$). Therefore a classification result which is very bad (equal to the probability of guessing, $cg=0$) and finishes only shortly before the *timeout*-boundary ($time=1$) would be as far as possible from this optimal point with $q_{new} = 1$ in this case.

The threshold for suitable classifiers is moved by the normalisation performed to the value of $1/\sqrt{2}$, i.e. classifiers that only guess at the result but do so very fast are located exactly at this boundary.

Summarising the benefits of this our new performance metric q_{new} we can say that:

- It takes the runtimes of the classifier/detector implementations into account, which is closer to the practical requirements for such a system (i.e. faster implementations would be preferred over slower implementations with the same detection power).
- It efficiently removes classifiers that are per definition unsuitable from the list of candidates by defining a timeout boundary for the execution time. Therefore evaluations are speed up.
- It allows for an intuitive performance description by using as a metric a normalised distance from an easy to understand "optimal" operation point.
- It allows for a direct comparison between classifications of different class-sizes (e.g. two-class problems and 4-class problems).

The drawbacks of this metric can be summarised as follows:

- It is dependent of the machine it is run on. This drawback could easily be compensated by computing a time correction factor between different machines to make their *runtime* results directly comparable.
- For the selection of methods for the implementation of a security mechanism, it would have to be accompanied by another value or set of values for precise throughput description (e.g. the processing speed in feature vectors per second – which could be given separately for training and testing in case the training can be performed a priori).
- It assumes (in the modelling of *probGuess*) that the classes in training are equally distributed.

All considerations have so far been made under the assumption that a single classifier is used to perform the steganalysis. For complex fusion information systems combining multiple classifiers into one steganalyser the considerations have to be extended. For the runtime consideration here the question arises whether the classifications are run in parallel or in sequence. In the first case, obviously the runtime of the slowest classifier in the fusion set defines the runtimes for the whole system. In the latter case the runtimes add up to the overall figure. Regarding the confidence/reliability of the fused decision the considerations are more complex. An accuracy of 100% in supervised classification does not tell much about the applicability of fused classifiers in real world investigations. Here, not only the accuracy of the involved classifiers have to be considered, but also a confidence has to be determined as a measure how far the fusion decision is away from the complex decision boundary of the overall fusion-based decision. In [29] some preliminary considerations on the modelling of such confidence estimation in a different context are made but in general this topic is still an open question for future research.

3.2 Plausibility of Decisions in an SPR-Based Steganalysis Setup

The throughput analysis introduced in section 3.1. acts as sine qua non for all further plausibility considerations. If no suitable classifier (or more precisely feature extractor and classifier combination) can be found – and suitable here implies a q_{new} significantly larger than $1/\sqrt{2}$ – all further considerations are pointless. But if at least one such a suitable classifier is found, further questions have to answered to establish trust in the decisions of this/these classifier(s). Here six of these further questions are considered, as already summarised in section 1.:

The **initial (or naïve) trust assumption** in our work is based on the detection performance of a classifier that fulfils the sine qua non – the requirement of a classification accuracy significantly larger than zero. In many publications (like e.g. [18] or [14]) this is done by (implicitly) using classification accuracies established in controlled evaluations as a means to specify the trust in the steganalyser. In section 3.1. of this paper we express our concerns against using the accuracy as a metric and introduce with the cg and q_{new} two new metrics that seem to be more appropriate to model an initial (or naïve) trust assumption. Actually, we would prefer using the q_{new} over the cg, due to the fact that it also considers the response time of the mechanism.

In many practical application fields, the **different error classes** that might be encountered have different consequences. For example, a biometric user authentication system run in verification mode has two distinct error cases: a false rejection rate (FRR) and a false acceptance rate (FAR). The significances for these two error classes are completely different: the false rejections are of concern for the usability of the system while the false acceptances are a security issue. Since biometric authentication systems are in the majority distance based template matching engines, here the decision threshold is directly influencing both error classes. If it is set very low (which is the case for high-security application scenarios), then the system shows a high false rejection rate but also a low false acceptance rate. If the decision threshold is very high, then we usually see a low false rejection rate but a high false acceptance rate. A typical system requirement specification in this field gives a relationship between these two error rates, like "must be better than 10^{-5} FAR at 10^{-3} FRR" (see e.g. the so called horizontal and vertical averaging in [32]).

The statistical pattern recognition based approaches used for most steganalysis approaches are to some extend similar to the biometric verification example used above. They are also a pattern recognition based security mechanism and they are also (in most cases) considered to be a two-class problem. Nevertheless, they lack such a parameterisable decision threshold that directly influences both error classes. Instead both error classes (statistical Type I and Type II errors – false positives and false negatives) have to be considered here as being independent. One trained classifier model is therefore assumed to display a fixed error ratio regarding the two possible classes. If multiple steganalysers (i.e. feature extractor, classifier and classifier model combinations) are considered for field application, it depends of the requirements for the application scenario which of these alternative steganalysers would be chosen. These requirements would include considerations on the throughput but also on the allowed false positives and false negatives – with high security scenarios strongly trying to minimise the number of false negatives.

In case the steganalysis problem at hand is not formulated as the typical two-class problem but instead aims at algorithm identification in an n-class problem the situation might become even more complex. In this case different levels of severity might be assigned to the different classes, e.g. based on the capacity that a different steganographic algorithms offer.

Another important question to be addressed here is the question about the **statistical generalisability** of the results at hand, considering known problems from classification (like overfitting) and required evaluation set sizes. The property of performing well on real-world data – which can be considered in this context to be equivalent to statistical generalisability – is commonly referred in the machine learning field as generalization [10]. A classifier which performs well on data outside of its training set is said to "generalize" well. This ability is an important goal to accomplish when designing a classifier.

It is important to supply the classifier with training data that is representative for the total possible space of inputs which it could encounter in real world situations. If the training data has been chosen poorly, it is likely that the classifiers will rely on features that only occur frequently in the training set and which are not useful in real world applications. Poorly chosen material can be distinguished into two classes: either the training samples are chosen from the range of values to be expected in real world application but there are not enough samples chosen to describe this domain completely (i.e. the training set size is not statistically significant), or, the training samples come (completely or partially) from outside the range of values to be expected in the real world application or do not present the representation of the target classes in this range appropriately.

It has to be understood that the complexity for training and application of classifier models is strongly dependent on the number of training samples used. Therefore it would be beneficial to keep the number of training samples as low as possible, which leads to the risk of choosing a too small set of training candidates in this optimisation problem. Here, investigations have to be made for each SPR-based security mechanism wow large the training set sizes have to be to allow for a suitable description of the problem domain while on the other hand preventing the model to become to large (high complexity in training and field application).

The other class of poorly chosen training material is describing the over-fitting problem. In over-fitting situations (which are the exact opposite of generalisation) the classifier is trained wrongly and is in practice only able to correctly recognise data from its training set [11]. The most important considerations to be performed here should focus between the correlation **between the training context and the application context**. The question behind these considerations is trying to address whether the steganalyser will only perform properly on material identical in its statistics to the statistics of the training context or whether the mechanism is capable of making successful decisions in a wider range of application contexts. In [9] we introduced the concepts of context dependent and content independent training and testing. In the cover signal specific steganalysis performed in [9] the classification results achieved for nine different information hiding algorithms show a rather strong impact of the correlation between the training and test set material for the considered SPR-based steganalyser.

In case signal operations of non-malicious nature have to be allowed for on the digital media objects under evaluation (which is a rather likely scenario in media-based communication, where much of the data undergoes a post processing prior to distribution) the generalisability considerations are made even more complicated. In the case where the **influence of non-malicious audio signal processing operations** on the steganalyser has to be considered, the range of the values representing "harmless" (non-stego objects) becomes statistically more complex by every additional allowed operation and also the distance between non-stego and stego objects assumably decreases, which makes the classification problem harder. The only option seems to be here to include such non-malicious signal processing operations into the evaluation of the steganalyser prior of its roll-out as a security mechanism.

One further point to consider is the **relevance of the features** used for the classification problem at hand. A classifier tends to learn the easiest features it can. A rather renowned story in the data mining community to illustrate this fact tells of scientists in a military project trying to train a neural network to classify images as containing either tanks or trees. Sometimes this possibly apocryphal story is told claiming to aim at the distinction between American and Russian tanks. The story is summarised in [12] as follows: scientists present pictures of trees and pictures of tanks to the neural network to train it. After sophisticated pre-processing of the images, these are fed in the neural network and, after considerable training, the network is able to classify each image correctly. However, when it is tested on other images, the network seems to classify every image as trees, even when it contains a tank. After careful study, the scientists finally resolve the mystery: in all the images used in the training, those containing trees were always taken in broad daylight, while those containing trees were always taken in a darker setting! Thus, the network had learned to distinguish the (trivial matter of) differences in overall light intensity rather than recognising the presence of tanks. Therefore the relevance of features looks for exactly these features that as precisely as possible divide the individual classes in the classification problem. Also, an optimal set of features would contain no redundancy, so the correlation between the features in such a set would be zero, to reduce the dimensionality of the classification problem and thereby enhance the throughput.

Relevance considerations on the features should also look into different feature types, which have a strong impact on the throughput. The two general types that are most commonly considered in this context in literature (e.g. [13]) are local and global features. Local as well as global features are either determined content based or without higher-level content analysis. A good example for content based local features is the determination of minutiae in fingerprint images; an example for local features computed without higher-level content analysis could be the colour-value distance between one pixel and the next in a row in an image. For content based global features an example could be the existence of a specific object (e.g. a tank) in an image; an example for global features computed without higher-level content analysis could be the entropy of a complete signal. It is obvious that the global features perform the strongest information reduction, while especially the local features computed without higher-level content analysis provide very little information reduction.

As an in-between for local and global features a third class, the segment-wise computed features (also known as segmental features or intra-window features) can be determined. They could be considered as being a global feature (e.g. entropy) applied only to a segment of the whole signal or as the evaluation of local features for a whole segment (e.g. the number of colour-value changes in and image block). Also this segmental approach to feature computation is often employed when features are extracted in a transform domain representation of the original signal (e.g. in frequency domain representations of audio or image signals) since many established domain transforms are working segment-wise (a.k.a. window-wise). Local features might be of use in media formats with a small number of data points (e.g. digital images, which are usually not larger than 10,000,000 data points or pixels) but their usage in high data rate media formats like audio or video is unfeasible, therefore they are removed from considerations within this paper focussed on audio steganalysis, although it has to be acknowledged here that local features are successfully used in image steganalysis [14].

Information **fusion** (sometimes also called ensemble methods) is trying to increase the decision performance of pattern recognitions mechanisms. The fusion or combination of experts can be done in two general ways: either by combining experts of different types (e.g. [1], [3]) or by using the same expert on different subsets of the feature space (e.g. [14]). While the first approach assumes that the classification problem can be represented and solved in low-dimensional feature spaces, the second approach assumes that the repeated, random dimensionality reduction and application of a base learner on different subspaces of the original space together with a decision based on the aggregation of the base learner outputs can solve an high dimensional classification problem efficiently [15]. The literature mentioned above (and further publications) have shown that information fusion can improve the detection accuracy of (ensemble) steganalysers, given suitable fusion operators and individual experts (or a suitable base learner in an appropriate high-dimensional feature space). Nevertheless, current research is still lacking an answer to the question how to model the trust in a decision generated by such an ensemble steganalyser.

3.3 Detector-Based Steganographic Channel Characterisation

If a steganalysis performing security mechanism would detect the presence of hidden channels in the data under observation, the statistical characteristics that lead to the detection could be used to characterise the steganographic channel. Information like the used embedding domain (e.g. [24]) and -strategy might be deduced and an algorithm identification (e.g. [16]) as well as key scenario considerations (e.g. [3]) and payload estimation (e.g. [23]) operations might be performed.

3.4 Countermeasures (i.e. Modifications on the Cover Channel)

Assuming a suitable steganalysis performing security mechanism could be implemented for a given cover channel, the next question to be addressed would be: How to react if the usage of steganography is detected?

In some application scenarios we might only have the possibility to disrupt the complete cover channel (passive warden scenario). In an active warden scenario more sophisticated measures might be found in filtering operations on the cover data to eliminate the embedded steganographic information (e.g. [26]).

Nevertheless, since steganography and steganalysis can be considered to constitute an each other influencing set of counter-sciences, it has to be assumed that steganographers are aware of possible countermeasures (see e.g. [25] on this topic).

4   Application of the Methodology and Concepts

This section briefly demonstrates the benefit of the application of our methodology and concepts in practice. The first part of the presented results shows in section 4.1 how the throughput of different supervised classifiers used for steganalysis can be compared using the q_{new} metric introduced in section 3.1. In section 4.2 selected considerations on the plausibility of our work on audio steganalysis are discussed.

4.1   Applied throughput Analysis

If we use our own evaluation results from [27] as input for the throughput analysis described in section 3.1., the performance of 74 different supervised classifiers (from the WEKA data mining suite [6]) on three different audio data hiding algorithms (called *AS1*, *AW1* and *AW3* – see [27] for details) can be visualised as shown in figures 1 and 2.

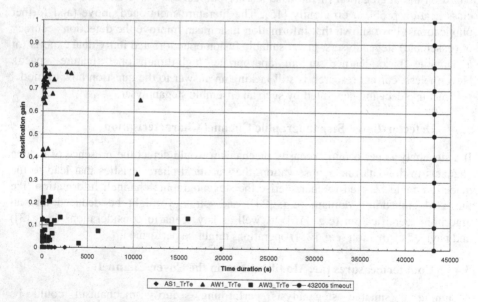

Fig. 1. Throughput analysis: training and testing with all 74 supervised classifiers in WEKA v.3.6.1 and three data hiding algorithms; classification gain over time - linear scale for the x-axis (diagram based on the classifier benchmarking results presented in [27])

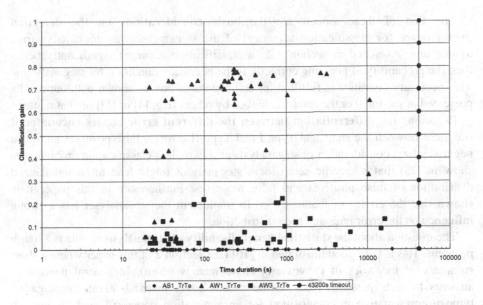

Fig. 2. Throughput analysis: training and testing with all 74 supervised classifiers in WEKA v.3.6.1 and three data hiding algorithms; classification gain over time - logarithmic scaling for the x-axis (diagram based on the classifier benchmarking results presented in [27])

In figure 1 the throughput is shown in a classification gain over time diagram. The "optimal" point, which would be a decision machine that gives a perfect classification (cg=1) in an extremely short time-span ($time$=0), is here the upper left corner of this diagram. Therefore the metric q_{new} introduced within this paper would be the absolute distance from this optimal point. As can be seen in figure 1 the three data hiding algorithms evaluated in [27] achieve extremely different throughput performances. The best results (with a smallest q_{new} of 0.1488 ($accuracy$=89.48% and $runtime$=230.1s) achieved by $weka.classifiers.functions.Logistic$) the best result is achieved for $AW1$.

The worst result in this diagram is achieved by a classifier that takes 19695s seconds for the training and classification for $AS1$ with $weka.classifiers.rules.NNge$ to come up with a classification accuracy of 50% in this 2-class problem (cg=0).

Since figure 1 does not allow for an easy comparison of the distribution of the results within the clusters representing the three evaluated data hiding algorithms, a logarithmically scaled version of this diagram is presented in figure 2.

4.2   Applied Plausibility Investigations

The six different aspects of the plausibility of steganalysis identified in section 1. for practical investigations are considered here and illustrated using our own research work in audio steganalysis.

The first of these aspects are the **basic considerations on the detection performance** (or classification accuracy) of the steganalysers as initial/naïve trust assumption. As stated in section 3.2., a classification accuracy significantly better then the probability of guessing correctly is the necessary condition for steganalysers. This necessary condition is fulfilled for audio steganalysis, as shown with our results presented in section 0 or the results achieved by others (e.g. [4] or [5]) on that matter.

Regarding the **differentiation between the different error classes encountered** (i.e. here between the statistical Type I and Type II errors – false positives and false negatives for a consideration of steganalysis as a two-class classification problem) we show in [28] that a specific setup for a steganalyser might lead to an unbalanced distribution of false positives and false negatives. Furthermore in this paper it is shown that the choice of features used to implement the steganalyser has a strong influence on the error rates and their distribution.

The question about the **statistical generalisability** of steganalysis results is a tough problem. This is very good illustrated in [16] (see section 2 of this paper where a short summary of the work of Provos and Honeyman is given). In general it requires answers to such questions like: "Is the chosen cover material for an investigation typical/representative in composition for an application scenario?" and "Is enough training and test material available/used?"

To answer the question about the representative context, we try to model the application context as closely as possible in the training of the classifiers as well as in the composition of the evaluation test sets. E.g. for analyses on VoIP steganalysis, where the typical cover data is human speech, we use speech data for training and evaluation. For general purpose audio steganalysis we generated a large multi-genre audio training set and a test set of similar composure (see e.g. [27] for details). To investigate whether the classifier shows overfitting tendencies, we compare in [27] results for 10-fold stratified cross-validation and training and testing on completely different sets of audio files, with the result that the discrepancies between the classification accuracies achieved imply how much overfitting takes place.

Regarding the question whether enough training and test material was used, our solution so far has been to increase the training set sizes until a stable level for the classification accuracy is reached.

The plausibility of steganalysis also has to look into the **influence of other (non-malicious) audio signal processing operations** on the classification behaviour of the steganalyser. The motivation for this consideration in found in the fact that especially pieces of music undergo rather dramatic modifications between their recording and the roll-out on a CD. One example for such modification is the custom to 'improve' singers voices with artificial reverberation. Table 1 shows the results of an experiment from [27] where we train classifiers for three different data hiding algorithms (*AS1*, *AW1* and *AW3*) and then apply these classifiers onto a completely unmarked audio material after non-malicious signal modifications (MP3 conversion and de-noising). For a complete description of the used evaluation setup we refer to [27].

Table 1. Classification accuracies (in %) for the global- (left column) and segmental features (right) and the best 5 classifiers from the classifier benchmarking in [27] for each algorithm (for a description of the used evaluation setup we refer to [27])

Mod.	Class.	AS1		AW1		AW3	
MP3 encoding	best	56.82	53.64	77.27	51.14	63.64	16.82
	2nd	56.82	9.09	70.45	76.93	95.45	71.14
	3rd	100	46.48	63.64	56.48	0	0
	4th	95.45	6.93	77.27	76.14	56.82	0
	5th	100	0	20.45	75.57	72.73	0
de-noising	best	29.55	53.97	100	99.88	79.55	96.14
	2nd	29.55	10.51	95.45	83.76	100	43.34
	3rd	100	50	84.09	65.07	100	0
	4th	100	1.75	90.91	71.03	100	0
	5th	100	0	100	77.57	100	0

A value of 100% in table 1 indicates that the complete test material was rightfully classified as unmarked by the corresponding feature extractor and classifier combination. A value of 0% means that the classifier produced false alarms on every input sample. Summarising these evaluation results it can be stated the de-noising operation output is in nine out of 15 test cases with the global features found 100% correct to be "not marked", in four other cases this value is above 80%, while for two cases are down to 29.55% equal to a rate of false alarms of 70.45%. For the MP3 encoding the picture is worse, with only two classifiers achieving 100% preciseness while all others show less than perfect results. One of the classifiers (the 3rd best for *AW3*) even shows a 100% false alarm rate.

It has to be stated that the segmental features perform significantly worse in these tests if it comes to plausibility against common signal modification operations. None of the 30 segmental test cases summarized in table 5 shows 100% preciseness, while eight cases show a false alarm rate of 100%.

In this investigation two different types of features are compared: global and segmental audio features. The choice which features to use influences, besides the classification accuracy achieved and the computational complexities of the feature extraction as well as the classification, also other questions, e.g. the localisation of modification/embeddings. While global features (which can be computed faster and which allow for faster classifications - see e.g. [27]), can only give an indication whether an audio signal is a stego object or not, segmental features could be used to identify which part of the file was modified and which was kept unchanged in case a low embedding strength (and a sequential embedding strategy) was used.

In general such considerations on features can be extended to investigations on whether **the features used for classification actually being relevant for the classification problem** at hand. Considering once more the work of Provos and Honeyman in [16], they notice from their investigations that Stegdetect shows a general tendency to classify unmarked drawings as stego objects generated with JSteg and images showing oil paints as output of Outguess 0.13b. To eliminate such wrongful global tendencies in our work we perform feature selection analyses under the assumption that these, if applied on the output of different steganographic tools, will allow us to estimate whether they are significant for steganographic embedding by certain algorithms or whether they are representing other content influences. For details see [24]. As additional benefits these feature selection investigations also allow us to group 'similar' algorithms, e.g. by their working domain, and decrease the dimensionality of the feature space used for classification and therefore increase the throughput.

Regarding investigations on the possibilities for increasing and estimating the decision performance by usage of **information fusion** by multiple steganalysers, it has to be stated that the few publications in this field for steganalysis show uniformly a rather non-satisfying picture. If the fusion considerations are only focussed on the feature spaces (e.g. [2] or [14]) then in nearly all cases a increase of the classification accuracies achieved is reported. If also other fusion levels are considered, like in the initial paper on this matter ([30]) or in our work on different fusion levels (e.g. [27]), then examples for increased as well as decreased classification accuracies are reported. A further remark for this topic has to be made on the increase in the computational complexity of the steganalysis task imposed by information fusion. Depending on the fusion level and fusion operator used, the increase in complexity can be either linear (on the number of fused steganalysers and observed material) or higher.

5   Summary and Conclusion

In this paper we on one hand introduce a throughput benchmarking scheme for steganalyser benchmarking and on the other hand we discuss plausibility considerations for steganalysers that aim to establish the trust that would be required in such a mechanism if it should ever be deployed for the detection of hidden communication channels in real world communication scenarios. The theoretical considerations presented here are accompanied with a brief practical demonstration on the applicability of our new benchmarking metric and the plausibility considerations in audio steganalysis research.

The next steps that will be considered in future work are extension of the considerations on benchmarking metrics into a fully developed and fair benchmarking scheme for practical steganalysis. We think that such benchmarking would be a necessity basis for large-scale usage in communication security. Similar fields of research on communication security already have benchmarking methods in place. Two examples for such initiatives to be mentioned here are the National Institute of Standards and Technology's (NIST, see http://www.nist.gov/itl/biometrics/index.cfm) work on Biometrics as well as the European Institute for Computer Antivirus Research (EICAR, see e.g. www.eicar.org/) with its work on malware detection.

Furthermore, additional plausibility related issues in this context have to be identified and considered in future work to further complete the picture considered.

References

[1] Kharrazi, M., Sencar, H.T., Memon, N.: Improving Steganalysis by Fusion Techniques: A Case Study with Image Steganography. In: Shi, Y.Q. (ed.) Transactions on Data Hiding and Multimedia Security I. LNCS, vol. 4300, pp. 123–137. Springer, Heidelberg (2006)

[2] Pevny, T., Fridrich, J.: Merging Markov and DCT Features for Multi-Class JPEG Steganalysis. In: Proc. SPIE EI Photonics West. IS&T/SPIE (2007)

[3] Kraetzer, C., Dittmann, J.: The Impact of Information Fusion in Steganalysis on the Example of Audio Steganalysis. In: Proceedings of the Media Forensics and Security XI, IS&T/SPIE 21st Annual Symposium on Electronic Imaging Conference, San Jose, CA, USA, January 18-22, vol. 7254 (2009)

[4] Ozer, H., Avcibas, I., Sankur, B., Memon, N.: Steganalysis of audio based on audio quality metrics. In: SPIE Electronic Imaging Conf. on Security and Watermarking of Multimedia Contents (2003)

[5] Ru, X.-M., Zhang, H.-J., Huang, X.: Steganalysis of audio: Attacking the steghide. In: Proceedings of the Fourth International Conference on Machine Learning and Cybernetics (2005)

[6] Hall, M., Frank, E., Holmes, G., Pfahringer, B., Reutemann, P., Witten, I.H.: The WEKA Data Mining Software: An Update. SIGKDD Explorations 11(1) (2009)

[7] Goljan, M., Fridrich, J., Holotyak, T.: New blind steganalysis and its implications. In: Delp, E.J., Wong, P.W. (eds.) Proceedings SPIE, Electronic Imaging, Security, Steganography, and Watermarking of Multimedia Contents VIII, San Jose, CA, January 16-19, vol. 6072, pp. 1–13 (2006)

[8] Cancelli, G., Doërr, G., Cox, I.J., Barni, M.: A comparative study of ±1 steganalyzers. In: Proceedings IEEE International Workshop on Multimedia Signal Processing, Cairns, Australia, October 8-10, pp. 791–796 (2008)

[9] Kraetzer, C., Dittmann, J.: Cover Signal Specific Steganalysis: the Impact of Training on the Example of two Selected Audio Steganalysis Approaches. In: Proceedings of the Security, Forensics, Steganography, and Watermarking of Multimedia Contents X, IS&T/SPIE 20th Annual Symposium on Electronic Imaging Conference, San Jose, CA, USA, January 26-31, vol. 6819 (2008)

[10] LeCun, Y.: Generalization and network design strategies. Technical Report CRG-TR-89-4, Department of Computer Science, University of Toronto (1989)

[11] Duda, R.O., Hart, P.E., Stork, D.G.: Pattern Classification: Pattern Classification Pt.1, 2nd edn. John Wiley & Sons (2000) ISBN-10: 9780471056690

[12] Bersano-Begey, T.F., Daida, J.M.: A Discussion on Generality and Robustness and a Framework for Fitness Set Construction in Genetic Programming to Promote Robustness. Stanford University, CA, USA (1997)

[13] Shyu, C.R., Brodley, C.E., Kak, A.C., Kosaka, A., Aisen, A., Broderick, L.: Local versus global features for content-based image retrieval. In: Proceedings of IEEE Workshop on Content-Based Access of Image and Video Libraries, Santa Barbara, CA, USA, June 21, pp. 30–34 (1998) ISBN: 0-8186-8544-1

[14] Kodovský, J., Fridrich, J.: Steganalysis in high dimensions: fusing classifiers built on random subspaces. In: SPIE, Electronic Imaging, Media Watermarking, Security, and Forensics XIII, San Francisco, CA, January 23-26 (2011)

[15] Kuncheva, L.I.: Combining Pattern Classifiers: Methods and Algorithms. Wiley-Interscience (2004)

[16] Provos, N., Honeyman, P.: Detecting Steganographic Content on the Internet. In: Proc. ISOC NDSS 2002, San Diego, CA (February 2002)

[17] Klein, D.: Foiling the Cracker: A Survey of, and Improvements to, Password Security. In: Proceedings of the 2nd USENIX Security Workshop, pp. 5–14 (August 1990)

[18] Farid, H.: Detecting Steganographic Messages in Digital Images. Technical Report TR2001-412, Deparment of Computer Science, Dartmouth College (August 2001)

[19] Fridrich, J., Du, R., Long, M.: Steganalysis of LSB Encoding in Color Images. In: Proceedings of the IEEE International Conference on Multimedia and Expo (August 2000)

[20] Givner-Forbes, R.: Steganography: Information Technology in the Service of the Jihad. A Report for the International Centre for Political Violence and Terrorism Research, Singapore (2007); Translated from "Secret Information: Hide Secrets Inside of Pictures" - unknown authorship in the Technical Mujahid, Issue 2 (March 2007), http://www.pvtr.org/pdf/Terrorism%20Informatics/Report_Ste ganography_final.pdf

[21] Kerckhoffs, A.: La cryptographie militaire. Journal des Sciences Militaires (Feburary 1883)

[22] Miche, Y., Roue, B., Lendasse, A., Bas, P.: A Feature Selection Methodology for Steganalysis. In: Gunsel, B., Jain, A.K., Tekalp, A.M., Sankur, B. (eds.) MRCS 2006. LNCS, vol. 4105, pp. 49–56. Springer, Heidelberg (2006)

[23] Fridrich, J., Goljan, M., Hogea, D., Soukal, D.: Quantitative Steganalysis of Digital Images: Estimating the Secret Message Length. ACM Multimedia Systems Journal, Special issue on Multimedia Security 9(3), 288–302 (2003)

[24] Kraetzer, C., Dittmann, J.: Impact of Feature Selection in Classification for Hidden Channel Detection on the Example of Audio Data Hiding. In: Proceedings of the 10th ACM Workshop on Multimedia and Security, Oxford, UK, September 22-23 (2008)

[25] Orsdemir, A., Altun, H.O., Sharma, G., Bocko, M.F.: Steganalysis-aware steganography: statistical indistinguishability despite high distortion. In: Proc. SPIE Symposium on Electronic Imaging, Security, Forensics, Steganography, and Watermarking of Multimedia Contents X, vol. 6819. IS&T (1999)

[26] Smith, C.B., Agaian, S.S.: Denoising and the active warden. In: Proc. IEEE International Conference on Systems, Man and Cybernetics 2007 (ISIC), Montreal, Que., Canada, October 7-10, pp. 3317–3322 (2007) ISBN: 978-1-4244-0991-4

[27] Kraetzer, C., Dittmann, J.: Improvement of information fusion-based audio steganalysis. In: Proceedings of Multimedia on Mobile Devices 2010, IS&T/SPIE 22nd Annual Symposium on Electronic Imaging Conference, San Jose, CA, USA, January 18-19, vol. 7542 (2010)

[28] Kraetzer, C., Dittmann, J.: Pros and Cons of Mel-cepstrum Based Audio Steganalysis Using SVM Classification. In: Furon, T., Cayre, F., Doërr, G., Bas, P. (eds.) IH 2007. LNCS, vol. 4567, pp. 359–377. Springer, Heidelberg (2008)

[29] Kraetzer, C., Schott, M., Dittmann, J.: Unweighted Fusion in Microphone Forensics using a Decision Tree and Linear Logistic Regression Models. In: Proceedings of the 11th ACM Workshop on Multimedia and Security, Princeton NJ, U.S.A., September 7-8 (2009)

[30] The Open Group: time a simple command. In Commands & Utilities Reference, The Single UNIX® Specification, The Open Group Base Specifications Issue 7, IEEE Standard 1003.1 (2008)

[31] Poh, N., Martin, A., Bengio, S.: Performance Generalization in Biometric Authentication Using Joint User-Specific and Sample Bootstraps. IEEE Transactions on Pattern Analysis and Machine Intelligence, 29(3), 492–498 (2007) ISSN: 0162-8828, doi: 10.1109/TPAMI.2007.55

[32] Carletta, J.: Assessing agreement on classification tasks: The kappa statistic. Computational Linguistics 22(2), 249–254 (1996)

[33] Gwet, K.: Handbook of Inter-Rater Reliability, 2nd edn. (2010) ISBN 978-0-9708062-2-2

[34] Di Eugenio, B., Glass, M.: The Kappa Statistic: A Second Look. Journal of Computational Linguistics 30(1) (March 2004)

Author Index